The Ukulele Songbook

Thomas Balinger

Ukulele in: **C**

Children's Songs Lullabies & Nursery Rhymes

Other titles by Thomas Balinger:

The Ukulele Songbook – 50 All Time Classics
The Ukulele Songbook – 50 All Time Classics, Vol. II
The Ukulele Songbook – Best of Gospel
The Ukulele Songbook – Hymns and Songs of Worship
The Ukulele Songbook – Christmas carols
The Ukulele Songbook – Shanties and Songs of the sea

Most wanted Ukulele Chords

Thomas Balinger
The Ukulele Songbook – Children's Songs, Lullabies & Nursery Rhymes

© 2016

ISBN: 978-1523426713

Preface

Dear parents,

do you still remember the songs you loved listening to as a kid?
Songs your parents used to sing when it was time to go to bed?
Have you ever wanted to sing these songs with your children and maybe
strum along a little on that Ukulele that's slowly collecting dust in the closet?
If the answer to one or all of the above is 'yes', this book's for you.

Whether you're a nursery teacher, a loving parent or just love making music
for children: on these pages, you'll find children's songs loved all around
the world in easy-to-play arrangements for Ukulele in standard C tuning
(G-C-E-A).
All songs in musical notation with chord symbols **plus** melody TAB – you
don't have to read music to start playing right away!

Whether you want to pick the melody, strum the chords or just need the
complete lyrics: you'll find everything you need on these pages. And if you
don't know how to play a particular chord, don't worry: each song features
easy-to-read chord diagrams, too.

For reference, there's a handy appendix listing basic chords plus a selection of
easy **strumming and picking patterns** you can use to accompany songs.

So pick up that Ukulele and dust off the strings!
Wishing you lots of fun with your Uke,

Thomas Balinger

Contents

Songs

Appendix

99 Bottles

Nine - ty - nine bot - tles of slime on the wall,

nine - ty - nine bot - tles of slime; _____ and

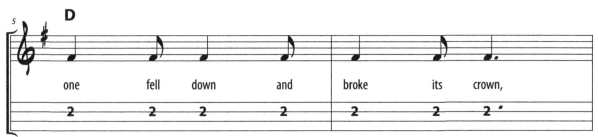

one fell down and broke its crown,

nine - ty - nine bot - tles of slime on the wall.

2. *98 bottles of slime on the wall,*
   98 bottles of slime.
   One fell down and broke its crown,
   98 bottles of slime on the wall.
etc.

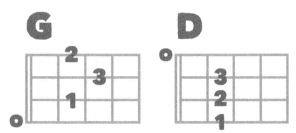

Amazing grace

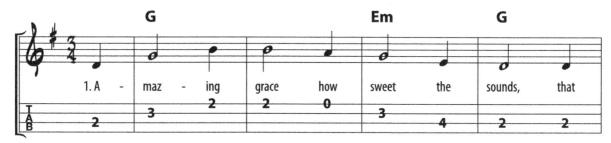

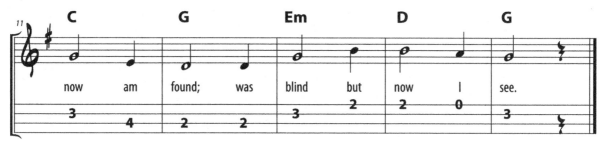

2. 'Twas grace that taught my heart to fear,
   And grace my fear relived.
   How precious did that grace appear,
   The hour I first believed.

3. When we've been there ten thousand years,
   Bright shining as the sun.
   We've no less days to sing God's praise,
   Than when we first begun.

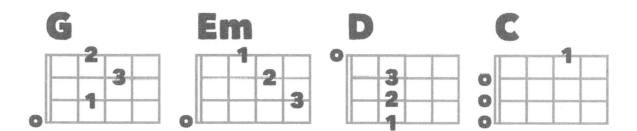

A-tisket, a-tasket

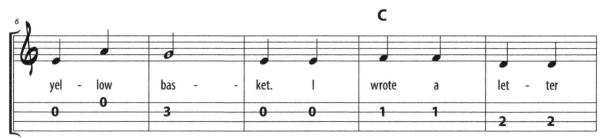

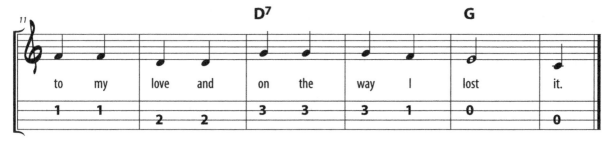

1. A-tisket a-tasket,
   a green and yellow basket,
   I wrote a letter to my love
   and on the way I lost it.

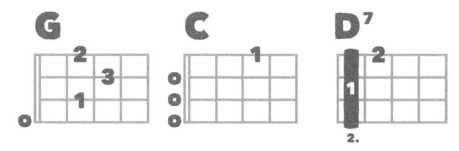

Hush, little baby

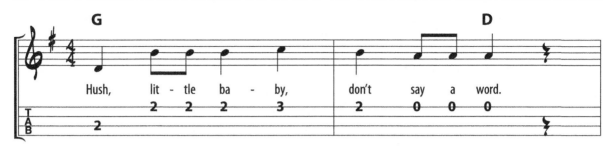

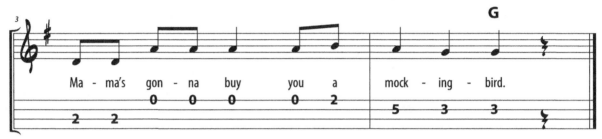

2. If that mockingbird won't sing,
   mama's gonna buy you a diamond ring

3. If that diamond ring turns brass,
   mama's gonna buy you a looking glass.

4. If that looking glass gets broke,
   mama's gonna buy you a billy goat,

5. If that billy goat don't pull,
   mama's gonna buy you a cart and bull.

6. If that cart and bull turn over,
   mama's gonna buy you a dog named Rover.

7. If that dog named Rover won't bark,
   mama's gonna buy you a horse and cart.

8. If that horse and cart fall down,
   you'll be the sweetest little baby in town.

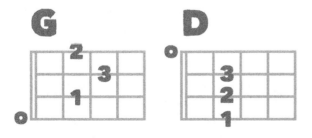

Pop goes the weasel

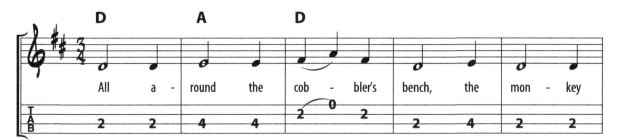

All a - round the cob - bler's bench, the mon - key

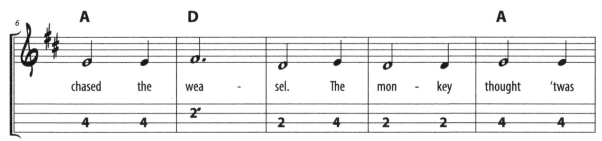

chased the wea - sel. The mon - key thought 'twas

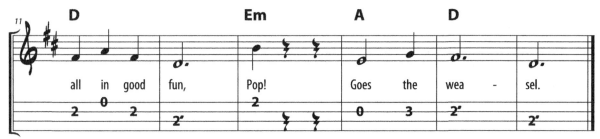

all in good fun, Pop! Goes the wea - sel.

2. A penny for a spool of thread,
   a penny for a needle.
   That's the way the money goes,
   Pop! Goes the weasel.

3. Jimmy's got the whooping cough
   and Timmy's got the measles.
   That's the way the story goes
   Pop! Goes the weasel.

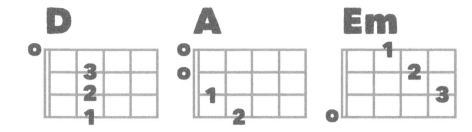

London Bridge is falling down

2. Take a key and lock her up,
lock her up, lock her up.
Take a key and lock her up,
my fair lady.

3. How will we build it up,
build it up, build it up?
How will we build it up,
my fair lady.

4. Build it up with gold and silver,
gold and silver, gold and silver.
Build it up with gold and silver,
my fair lady.

5. Gold and silver I have none,
I have none, I have none.
Gold and silver I have none,
my fair lady.

6. Build it up with needles and pins,
needles and pins, needles and pins.
Build it up with needles and pins,
my fair lady.

7. Pins and needles bend and break,
bend and break, bend and break.
Pins and needles bend and break,
my fair lady.

8. Build it up with wood and clay,
wood and clay, wood and clay.
Build it up with wood and clay,
my fair lady.

9. Wood and clay will wash away,
wash away, wash away.
wood and clay will wash away,
my fair lady.

10. Build it up with stone so strong,
stone so strong, stone so strong.
Build it up with stone so strong,
my fair lady.

11. Stone so strong will last so long,
last so long, last so long.
Stone so strong will last so long,
my fair lady.

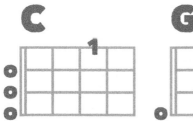

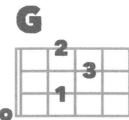

One elephant went out

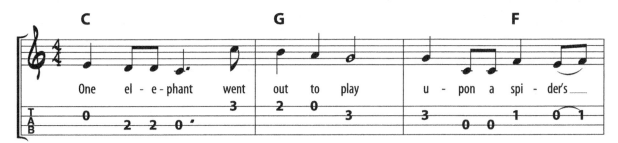

One el-e-phant went out to play u-pon a spi-der's___

web one day. He had such tre-men-dous fun that he

called for an-oth-er el-e-phant to come!

2. Two Elephants went out to play upon a spider's web one day.
   They had such tremendous fun that they called for another Elephant to come!

3. Three Elephants went out to play upon a spider's web one day.
   They had such tremendous fun that they called for another Elephant to come!

4. Four Elephants went out to play upon a spider's web one day.
   They had such tremendous fun that they called for another Elephant to come!

5. Five Elephants went out to play upon a spider's web one day.
   They had such tremendous fun that they all had a picnic in the sun!

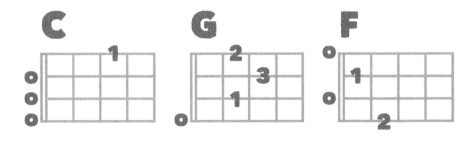

Rain, rain go away

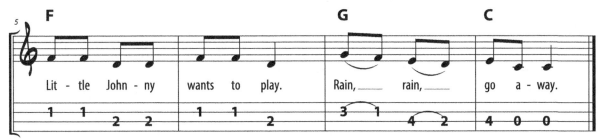

2. Rain, rain, go away,
   Come again another day.
   DADDY wants to play.
   Rain, rain, go away

3. Rain, rain, go away,
   Come again another day.
   MOMMY wants to play
   Rain, rain, go away.

5. Rain, rain, go away,
   Come again another day.
   BROTHER wants to play.
   Rain, rain, go away.

6. Rain, rain, go away,
   Come again another day.
   SISTER wants to play.
   Rain, rain, go away.

7. Rain, rain, go away,
   Come again another day.
   BABY wants to play
   Rain, rain, go away.

8. Rain, Rain, go away,
   Come again another day.
   ALL THE FAMILY wants to play.
   Rain, rain, go away.

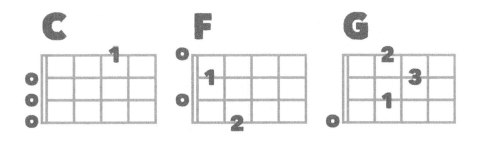

Polly wolly doodle

2. Oh, my Sal, she is a maiden fair,
   singing Polly wolly doodle all the day.
   With curly eyes and laughing hair,
   singing Polly wolly doodle all the day.
   Fare thee well ...

3. Behind the barn, down on my knees,
   singing Polly wolly doodle all the day.
   I thought I heard a chicken sneeze,
   singing Polly wolly doodle all the day.
   Fare thee well ...

4. He sneezed so hard with the whooping cough,
   singing Polly wolly doodle all the day.,
   He sneezed his head and the tail right off,
   singing Polly wolly doodle all the day.
   Fare thee well...

5. Oh, a grasshopper sittin' on a railroad track,
   singing Polly wolly doodle all the day.
   A-pickin' his teeth with a carpet tack,
   singing Polly wolly doodle all the day
   Fare thee well ...

6. Oh, I went to bed but it wasn't any use,
   singing Polly wolly doodle all the day.
   My feet stuck out like a chicken roost,
   singing Polly wolly doodle all the day
   Fare thee well ...

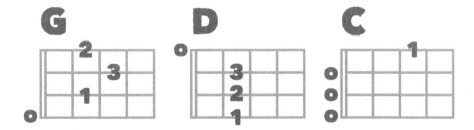

Lavender's blue

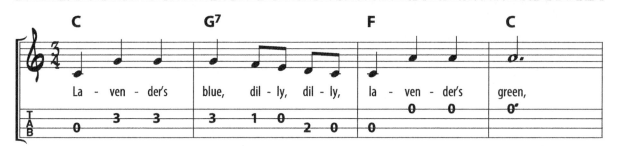

Lavender's blue, dilly, dilly, lavender's green,

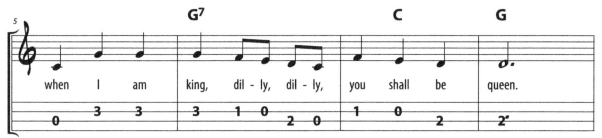

when I am king, dilly, dilly, you shall be queen.

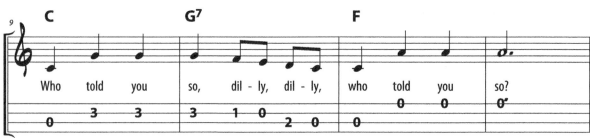

Who told you so, dilly, dilly, who told you so?

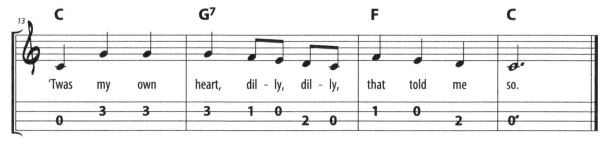

'Twas my own heart, dilly, dilly, that told me so.

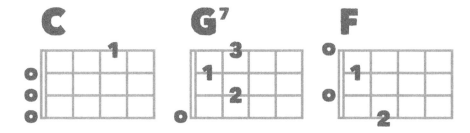

2. *Call up your men, dilly, dilly, set them to work*
   Some to the plough, dilly, dilly, some to the fork,
   some to make hay, dilly, dilly, some to cut corn,
   while you and I, dilly, dilly, keep ourselves warm.

3. *Lavender's green, dilly, dilly, Lavender's blue,*
   if you love me, dilly, dilly, I will love you.
   Let the birds sing, dilly, dilly, and the lambs play;
   we shall be safe, dilly, dilly, out of harm's way.

4. *I love to dance, dilly, dilly, I love to sing;*
   when I am queen, dilly, dilly, you'll be my king.
   Who told me so, dilly, dilly, who told me so?
   I told myself, dilly, dilly, I told me so.

Hickory dickory dock

C

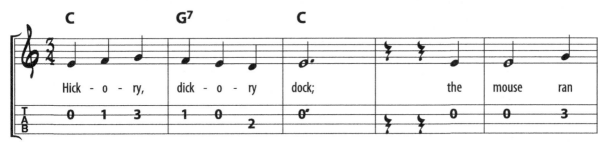

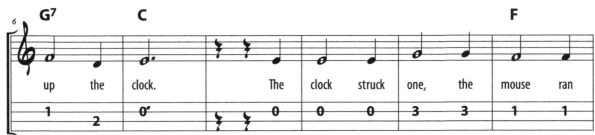

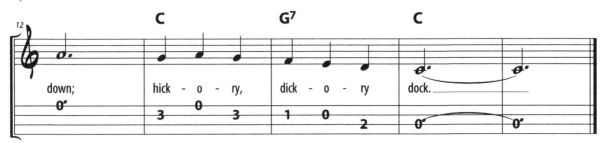

2. Hickory dickory dock,
   the mouse ran up the clock,
   the clock struck two
   and down he flew,
   hickory dickory dock.

3. Hickory dickory dock,
   the mouse ran up the clock,
   the clock struck three
   and he did flee,
   hickory dickory dock.

4. Hickory dickory dock,
   the mouse ran up the clock,
   the clock struck four,
   he hit the floor,
   hickory dickory dock.

5. Hickory dickory dock,
   the mouse ran up the clock,
   the clock struck five,
   the mouse took a dive,
   hickory dickory dock.

6. Hickory dickory dock,
   the mouse ran up the clock,
   the clock struck six,
   that mouse, he split,
   hickory dickory dock.

7. Hickory dickory dock,
   the mouse ran up the clock,
   the clock struck seven,
   8, 9, 10, 11,
   hickory dickory dock.

8. Hickory dickory dock,
   the mouse ran up the clock,
   as twelve bells rang,
   the mousie sprang,
   hickory dickory dock.

9. Hickory dickory dock,
   "Why scamper?" asked the clock,
   "You scare me so
   I have to go!"
   hickory dickory dock.

C

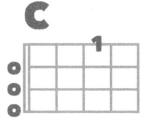

G⁷

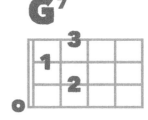

Teddy bear

2. Teddy bear, teddy bear, turn around!
Teddy bear, teddy bear, touch the ground!
Teddy bear, teddy bear, jump up high!
Teddy bear, teddy bear, touch the sky!

3. Teddy bear, teddy bear, bend down low!
Teddy bear, teddy bear, touch you toes!
Teddy bear, teddy bear, turn out the light!
Teddy bear, teddy bear, say good night!

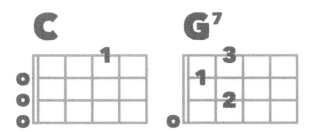

Rock-a-bye, baby

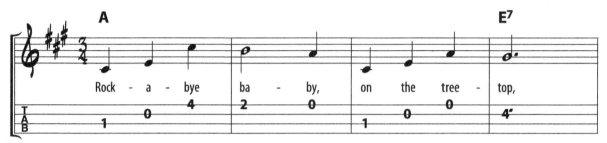

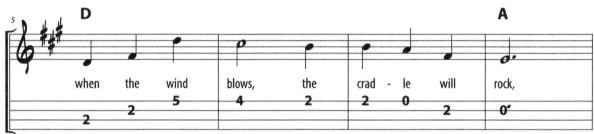

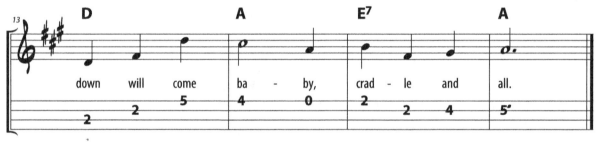

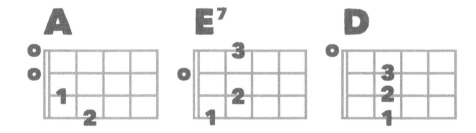

Itsy-bitsy spider

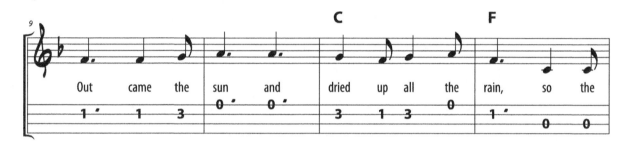

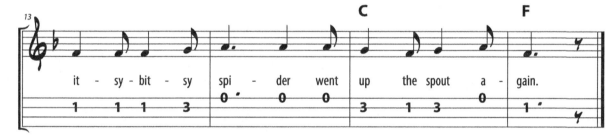

2. The great big spider went up the water spout ...

3. The teeny tiny spider went up the water spout ...

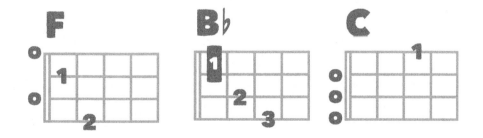

Crawdad song

2. Sittin' on the bank 'til my feet get cold, Honey.
Sittin' on the bank 'til my feet get cold, Baby.
Sittin' on the bank 'til my feet get cold,
lookin' down that crawdad hole, Honey, Baby mine.

3. Yonder comes a man with a sack on his back, Honey.
Yonder comes a man with a sack on his Baby.
Yonder comes a man with a sack on his back,
packin' all the crawdads he can pack, Honey, Baby mine.

4. The man fell down and he broke that sack, Honey.
The man fell down and he broke that sack, Baby.
The man fell down and he broke that sack,
see those crawdads backing back, Honey, Baby mine.

5. I heard the duck say to the drake, honey, honey.
I heard the duck say to the drake, baby, baby.
I heard the duck say to the drake,
there ain't no crawdads in this lake, Honey, Baby mine.

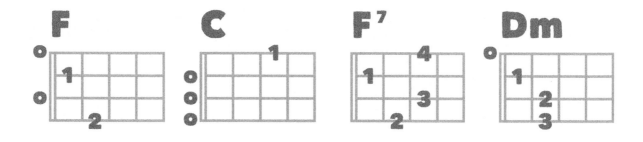

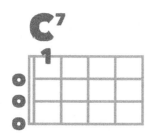

Baa, baa, black sheep

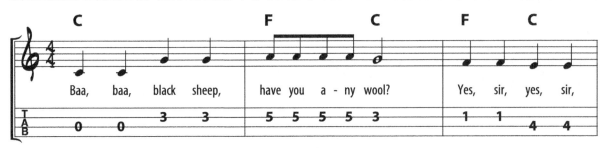

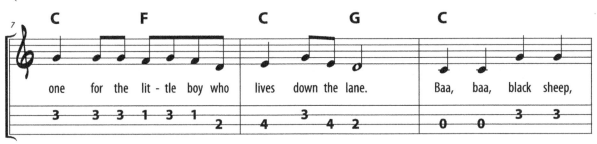

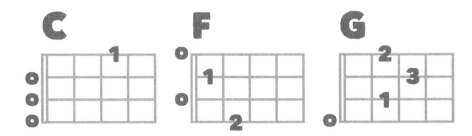

Bingo

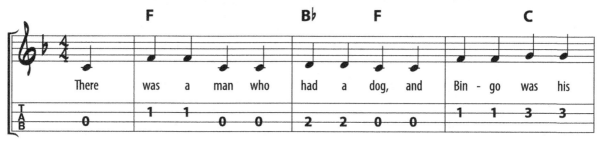

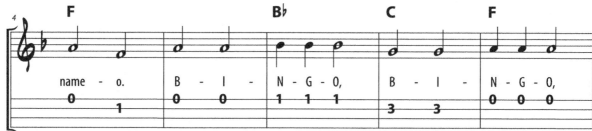

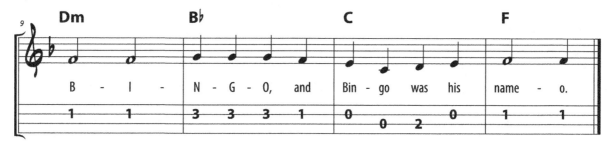

2. There was a man who had a dog,
   and Bingo was his name-o.
   (clap)-I-N-G-O (3x)
   and Bingo was his name-o.

3. There was a man who had a dog,
   and Bingo was his name-o.
   (clap)-(clap)-N-G-O (3x)
   and Bingo was his name-o.

4. There was a man who had a dog,
   and Bingo was his name-o.
   (clap)-(clap)-(clap)-G-O (3x)
   and Bingo was his name-o.

5. There was a man who had a dog,
   and Bingo was his name-o.
   (clap)-(clap)-(clap)-(clap)-O (3x)
   and Bingo was his name-o.

6. There was a man who had a dog,
   and Bingo was his name-o.
   (clap)-(clap)-(clap)-(clap)-(clap) (3x)
   and Bingo was his name-o.

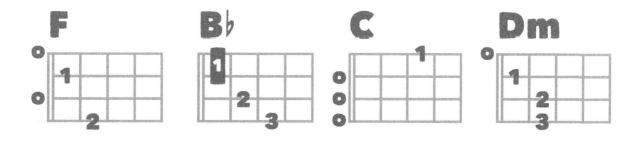

Brahms' Lullaby

Lull - a - by, and good night, with ___ pink ros - es

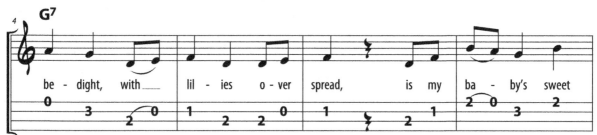

be - dight, with ___ lil - ies o - ver spread, is my ba - by's sweet

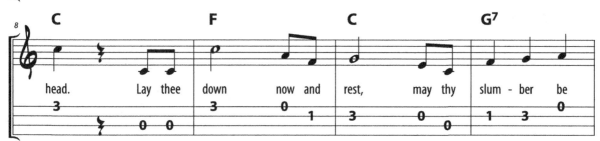

head. Lay thee down now and rest, may thy slum - ber be

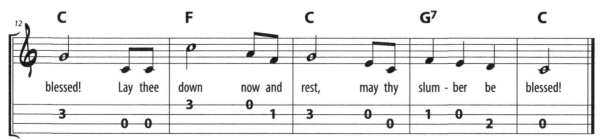

blessed! Lay thee down now and rest, may thy slum - ber be blessed!

2. Lullaby, and good night, your mother's delight,
   shining angels beside my darling abide.
   Soft and warm is your bed,
   close your eyes and rest your head.
   Soft and warm is your bed,
   close your eyes and rest your head.

3. Sleepyhead, close your eyes,
   mother's right here beside you.
   I'll protect you from harm,
   you will wake in my arms.
   Guardian angels are near,
   so sleep on, with no fear.
   Guardian angels are near,
   so sleep on, with no fear.

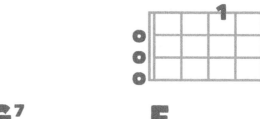

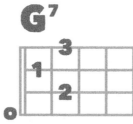

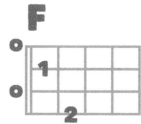

Jack and Jill

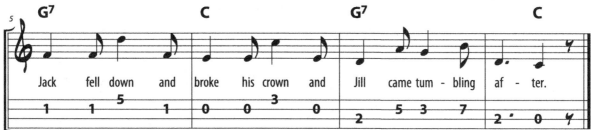

2. Up Jack got and home did trot,
   as fast as he could caper;
   and went to bed and bound his head
   with vinegar and brown paper.

3. When Jill came in how she did grin
   to see Jack's paper plaster;
   mother vexed did whip her next
   for causing Jack's disaster.

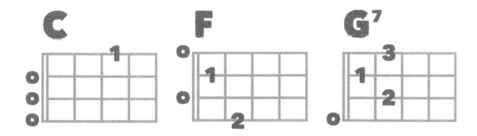

This old man

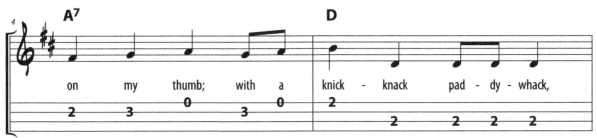

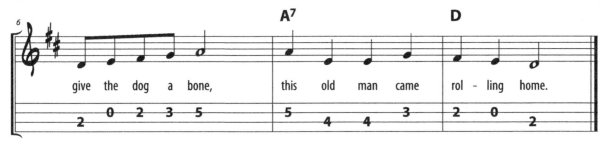

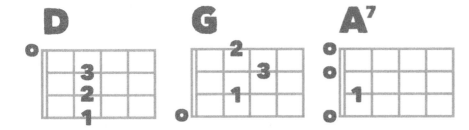

2. *This old man, he played two,*
   he played knick-knack on my shoe;
   with a knick-knack paddywhack,
   give the dog a bone,
   this old man came rolling home.

3. *This old man, he played three,*
   he played knick-knack on my knee;
   with a knick-knack paddywhack,
   give the dog a bone,
   this old man came rolling home.

4. *This old man, he played four,*
   he played knick-knack on my door;
   with a knick-knack paddywhack,
   give the dog a bone,
   this old man came rolling home.

5. *This old man, he played five,*
   he played knick-knack on my hive;
   with a knick-knack paddywhack,
   give the dog a bone,
   this old man came rolling home.

6. *This old man, he played six,*
   he played knick-knack on my sticks;
   with a knick-knack paddywhack,
   give the dog a bone,
   this old man came rolling home.

7. *This old man, he played seven,*
   he played knick-knack up in heaven;
   with a knick-knack paddywhack,
   give the dog a bone,
   this old man came rolling home.

8. *This old man, he played eight,*
   he played knick-knack on my gate;
   with a knick-knack paddywhack,
   give the dog a bone,
   this old man came rolling home.

9. *This old man, he played nine,*
   he played knick-knack on my spine;
   with a knick-knack paddywhack,
   give the dog a bone,
   this old man came rolling home.

10. *This old man, he played ten,*
    he played knick-knack once again;
    with a knick-knack paddywhack,
    give the dog a bone,
    this old man came rolling home.

J. J. J. Schmidt

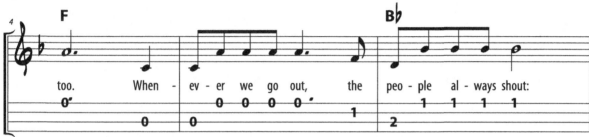

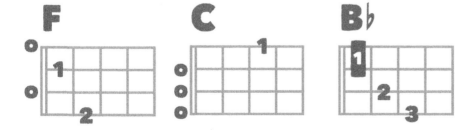

Little green frog

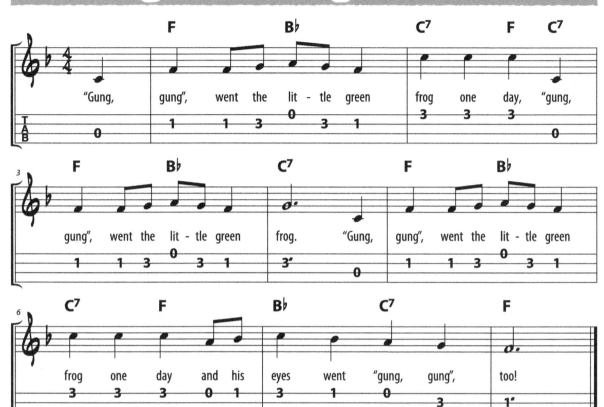

"Gung, gung", went the lit - tle green frog one day, "gung, gung", went the lit - tle green frog. "Gung, gung", went the lit - tle green frog one day and his eyes went "gung, gung", too!

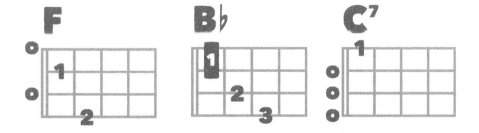

Camptown Races

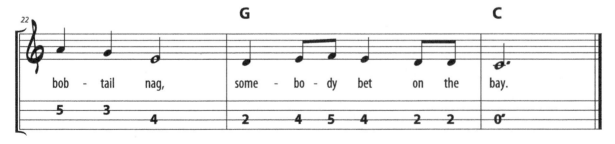

2. De long tail filly and de big black hoss, Doo-dah! doo-dah!
   Dey fly de track and dey both cut across, Oh, doo-dah-day!
   De blind hoss sticken in a big mud hole, Doo-dah! doo-dah!
   Can't touch bottom wid a ten foot pole, Oh, doo-dah-day

Refrain

3. Old muley cow come on to de track, Doo-dah! doo-dah!
   De bob-tail fling her ober his back, Oh, doo-dah-day!
   Den fly along like a rail-road car, Doo-dah! doo-dah!
   Runnin' a race wid a shootin' star, Oh, doo-dah-day!

Refrain

4. See dem flyin' on a ten mile heat, Doo-dah doo-dah!
   Round de race track, den repeat, Oh, doo-dah-day!
   I win my money on de bob-tail nag, Doo-dah! doo-dah!
   I keep my money in an old tow-bag, Oh, doo-dah-day!

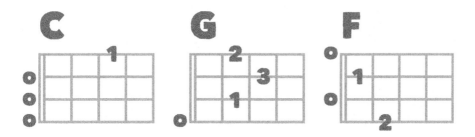

Marianne

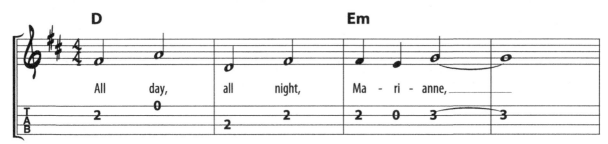

All day, all night, Ma - ri - anne,

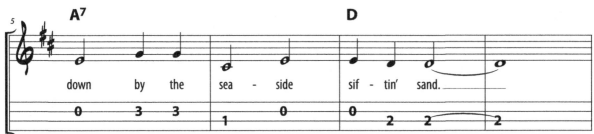

down by the sea - side sif - tin' sand.

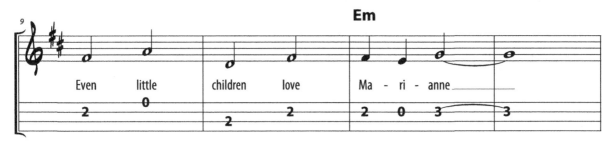

Even little children love Ma - ri - anne

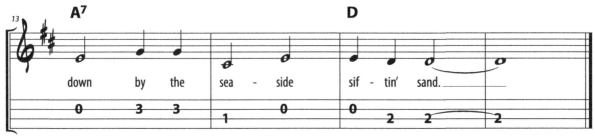

down by the sea - side sif - tin' sand.

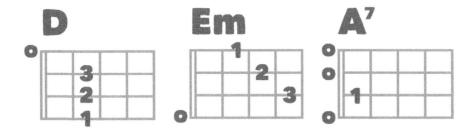

Good morning

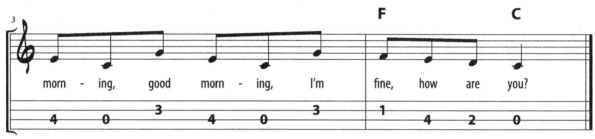

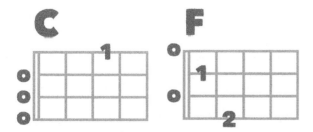

If you're happy

2. ... stomp your feet (stomp, stomp)

3. ... slap your legs (slap slap)

4. ... slap your knees (slap slap)

5. ... nod your head (nod nod)

6. ... tap your toe (tap tap)

7. ... honk your nose (honk honk)   etc.

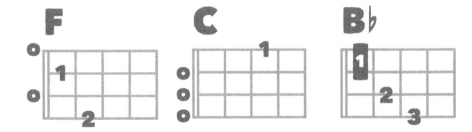

Hey, diddle, diddle

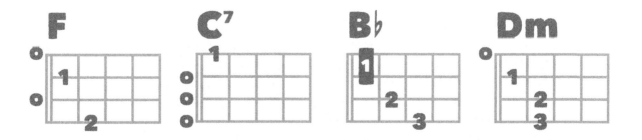

Old MacDonald had a farm

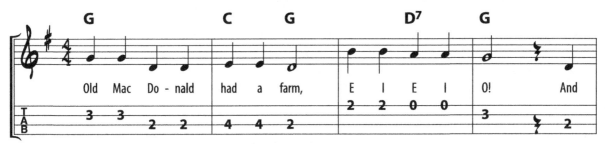

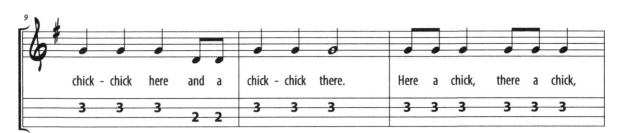

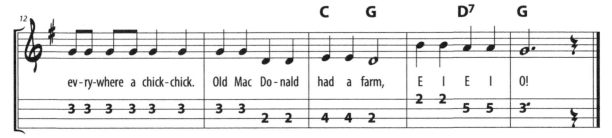

2. ... he had some geese ...
   With a gabble-gabble here ...

4. ... he had some ducks ...
   With a quack-quack here ...

3. ... he had a pig ...
   With a oinck-oink here ...

5. ... he had a cow ...
   With a moo-moo here ...

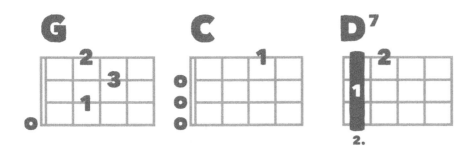

Sleep, baby, sleep

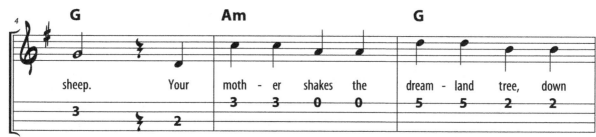

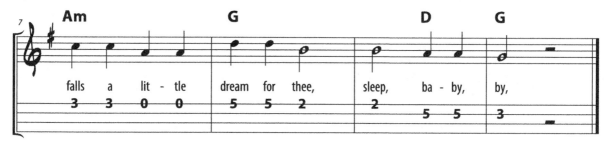

2. Sleep, baby, sleep.
   Your father guards the sheep.
   Your mother shakes the dreamland tree,
   down falls a little dream for thee,
   Sleep, baby, sleep.

3. Sleep, baby, sleep.
   Your father watches the sheep.
   The wind is blowing fierce and wild,
   it must not wake my little child.
   Sleep, baby, sleep.

4. Sleep, baby sleep.
   The large stars are the sheep.
   The little stars are the lambs, I guess,
   the gentle moon's the shepherdess.
   Sleep, baby, sleep.

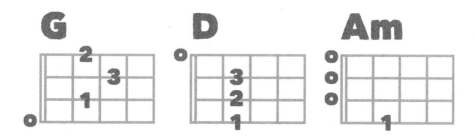

There's a hole in the bucket

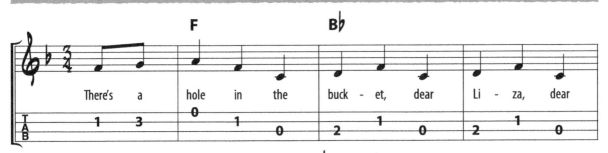

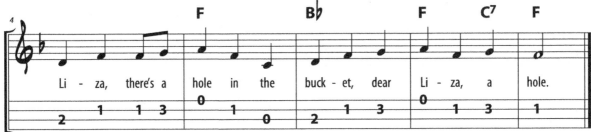

2. *Then fix it, dear Henry, dear Henry, dear Henry,*
   then fix it, dear Henry, dear Henry, fix it.

3. *With what shall I fix it, dear Liza, dear Liza?*
   with what shall I fix it, dear Liza, with what?

4. *With straw, dear Henry, dear Henry, dear Henry,*
   With straw, dear Henry, dear Henry, with straw.

5. *The straw is too long, dear Liza, dear Liza,*
   the straw is too long, dear Liza, too long.

6. *Then cut it, dear Henry, dear Henry, dear Henry,*
   then cut it, dear Henry, dear Henry, cut it.

7. *With what shall I cut it, dear Liza, dear Liza?*
   With what shall I cut it, dear Liza, with what?

8. *With a knife, dear Henry, dear Henry, dear Henry,*
   with a knife, dear Henry, dear Henry, with a knife.

9. *The knife is too dull, dear Liza, dear Liza,*
   the knife is too dull, dear Liza, too dull.

10. *Then sharpen it, dear Henry, dear Henry, dear Henry,*
    then sharpen it, dear Henry, dear Henry, sharpen it.

11. On what shall I sharpen it, dear Liza, dear Liza?
    On what shall I sharpen it, dear Liza, on what?

12. On a stone, dear Henry, dear Henry, dear Henry,
    on a stone, dear Henry, dear Henry, a stone.

13. The stone is too dry, dear Liza, dear Liza,
    the stone is too dry, dear Liza, too dry.

14. Then wet it, dear Henry, dear Henry, dear Henry,
    then wet it, dear Henry, dear Henry, wet it.

15. With what shall I wet it, dear Liza, dear Liza?
    With what shall I wet it, dear Liza, with what?

16. Try water, dear Henry, dear Henry, dear Henry,
    try water, dear Henry, dear Henry, water.

17. In what shall I fetch it, dear Liza, dear Liza?
    In what shall I fetch it, dear Liza, in what?

18. In the bucket, dear Henry, dear Henry, dear Henry,
    In the bucket, dear Henry, dear Henry, a bucket.

19. But there's a hole in my bucket, dear Liza, dear Liza,
    there's a hole in my bucket, dear Liza, a hole.

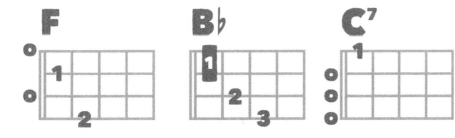

Silent night

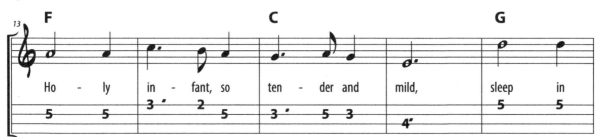

2. Silent night, Holy night!
   Son of God, love's pure light.
   Radiant beams from thy holy face.
   With the dawn of redeeming grace,
   Jesus, Lord at thy birth,
   Jesus, Lord at thy birth.

3. Silent night, Holy night!
   Shepherds quake, at the sight.
   Glories stream from heaven above.
   Heavenly, hosts sing Hallelujah,
   Christ the Savior is born,
   Christ the Savior is born.

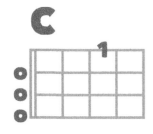

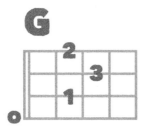

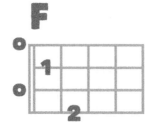

Skip to my Lou

2. There's a little red wagon, Paint it blue.

3. Lost my partner, What'll I do?

4. I'll get another one, Prettier than you.

5. Can't get a red bird, Jaybird'll do.

6. Cat's in the cream jar, Ooh, ooh, ooh.

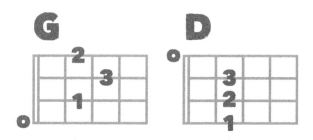

Twinkle, twinkle little Star

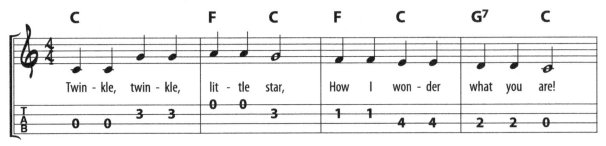

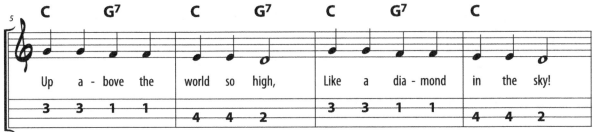

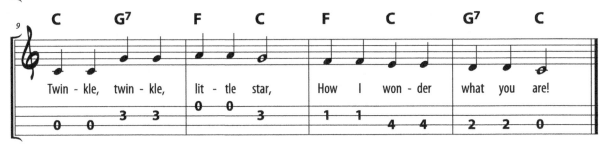

2. When the blazing sun is gone,
   When he nothing shines upon,
   Then you show your little light,
   Twinkle, twinkle, all the night.

3. Then the traveller in the dark,
   Thanks you for your tiny spark,
   He could not see which way to go,
   If you did not twinkle so.

4. In the dark blue sky you keep,
   And often through my curtains peep,
   For you never shut your eye,
   Till the sun is in the sky.

5. As your bright and tiny spark,
   Lights the traveller in the dark,
   Though I know not what you are,
   Twinkle, twinkle, little star.

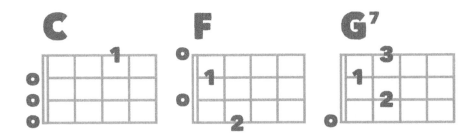

What shall we do with the drunken sailor

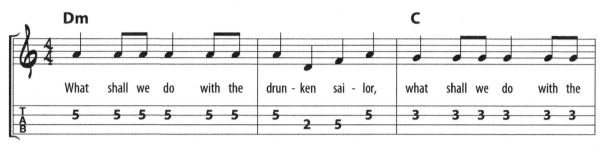

2. Give him a dose of salent water, early ...
3. Give him a dash with a besoms rubber, early ...
4. Pull out the plug and wet him all over, early ...
5. Heave him by the leg in a running bowlin', early ...
6. That's what to do with a drunken sailor, early ...

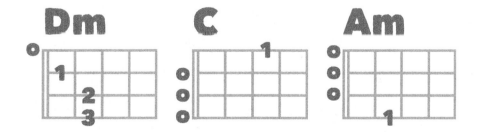

Jingle Bells

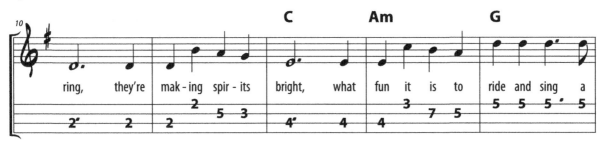

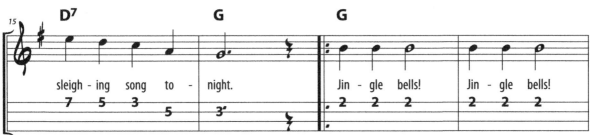

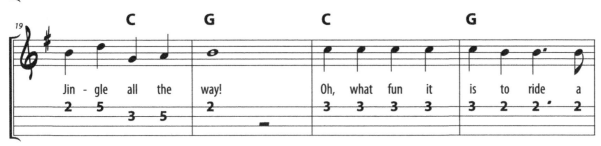

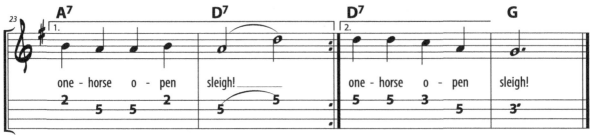

2. *A day or two ago I thought I'd take a ride,*
   And soon Miss Fannie Bright was seated by my side.
   The horse was lean and lank, misfortune seemed his lot,
   He got into a drifted bank and we got upsot.

3. *A day or two ago, The story I must tell*
   I went out on the snow, And on my back I fell;
   A gent was riding by In a one-horse open sleigh,
   He laughed as there I sprawling lie, But quickly drove away.

4. *Now the ground is white, go it while you're young,*
   Take the girls tonight and sing this sleighing song.
   Just get a bobtailed bay, two-forty for his speed,
   Then hitch him to an open sleigh, and crack! You'll take the lead.

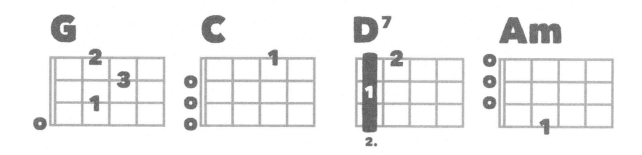

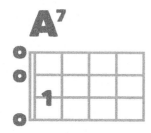

Brother John

F

Are you sleep - ing? Are you sleep - ing? Broth - er John,

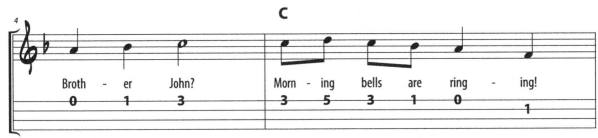

Broth - er John? Morn - ing bells are ring - ing!

C

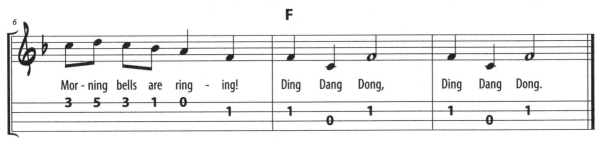

Mor - ning bells are ring - ing! Ding Dang Dong, Ding Dang Dong.

F

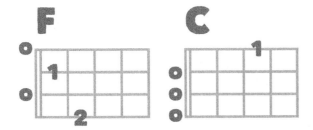

She'll be coming round the mountain

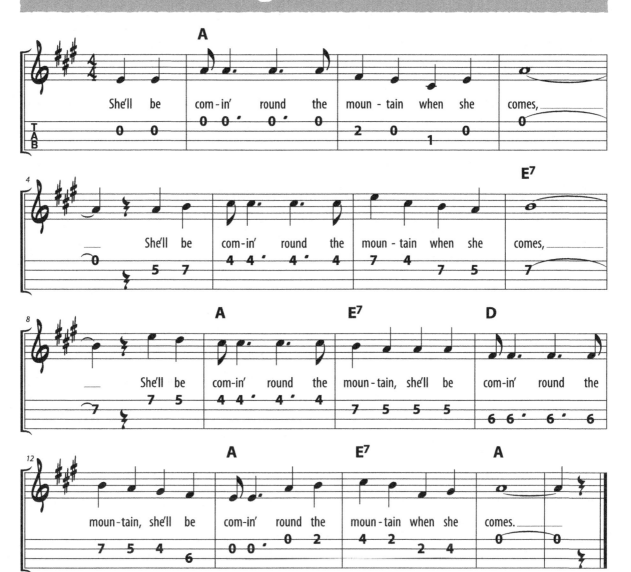

2. She'll be driving' six white horses when she comes ...
3. We will all go out to meet her when she comes ...
4. We will have chickden an' dumplin's when she comes ...
5. She'll be reelin' an' a-rockin' when she comes ...
6. We'll shout glory hallelujah when she comes ...

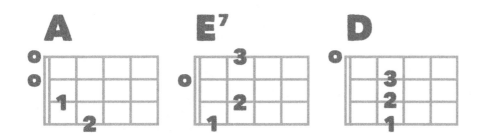

Yankee Doodle

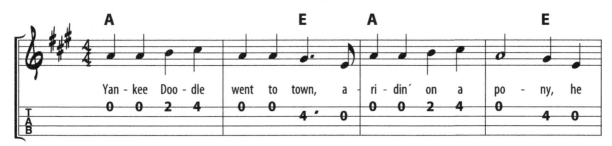

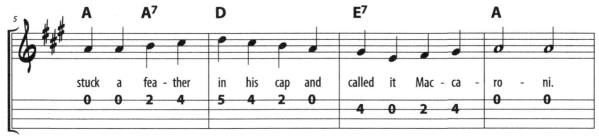

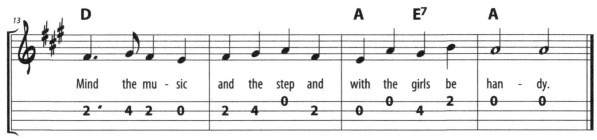

2. *Father and I went down to camp,*
   along with Captain Gooding.
   And there we saw the men and boys,
   as thick as hasty pudding.
   Yankee Doodle, keep it up,
   Yankee Doodle dandy.
   Mind the music and the step,
   and with the girls be handy.

3. *There was Captain Washington,*
   upon a slapping stallion.
   A-giving orders to his men,
   I guess there was a million.
   Yankee Doodle, keep it up,
   Yankee Doodle dandy.
   Mind the music and the step,
   and with the girls be handy.

4. *Yankee Doodle is a tune,*
   that comes in mighty handy,
   The enemies all run away,
   at Yankee Doodle Dandy!
   Yankee Doodle, keep it up,
   Yankee Doodle dandy.
   Mind the music and the step,
   and with the girls be handy.

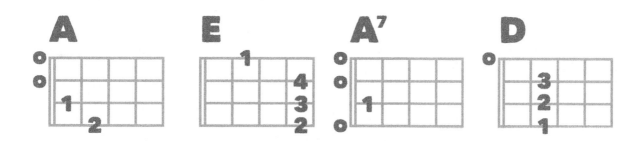

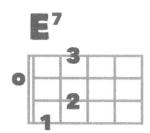

Clementine

2. *Light she was, and like a fairy,*
   and her shoes were number nine,
   herring boxes without topses,
   sandals were for Clementine

3. *Drove she ducklings to the water*
   every morning just at nine,
   struck her foot agains a splinter,
   fell into the foaming brine.

4. *Rosy lips above the water,*
   blowing bubbles mighty fine,
   but, alas, I was no swimmer,
   so I lost my Clementine.

5. *How I missed her! How I missed her!*
   How I missed my Clementine!
   But I kissed her little sister,
   and forgot my Clementine.

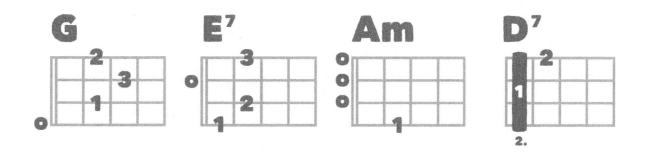

Go, tell it on the mountain

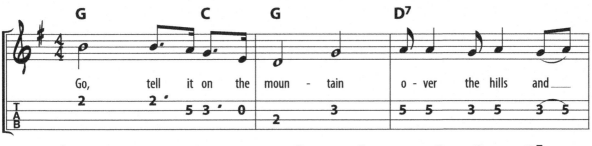

2. He made me a watchman upon the city-wall,
   and if I am a christian I am the least of all.

3. 'T was a lowly manger that Jesus Christ was born.
   The Lord sent down an angel that bright and glorious morn'.

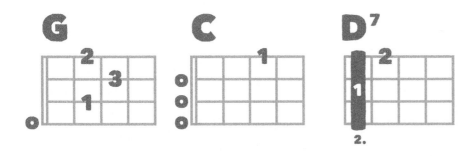

The bear went over the mountain

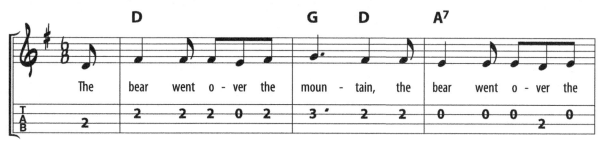

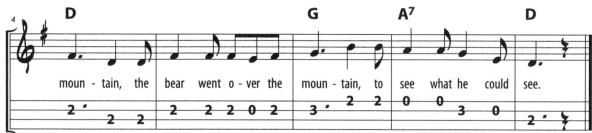

2. The other side of the mountain,
   the other side of the mountain,
   the other side of the mountain,
   was all that he could see.

3. The bear went over the river,
   the bear went over the river,
   the bear went over the river,
   to see what he could see.

4. The other side of the river,
   the other side of the river,
   the other side of the river,
   was all that he could see.

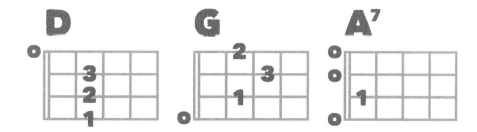

Oh Susanna

2. I had a dream the other night
when ev'rything was still;
I thought I saw Susanna
a-comin' down the hill;
the buckwheat cake was in her mouth,
the tear was in her eye;
says I, I'm comin' from the south,
Susanna, don't you cry.
O, Susanna,
o, don't you cry for me ...

3. I soon will be in New Orleans,
and then I'll look around,
and when I find Susanna
I'll fall upon the ground.
And if I do not find her,
then I will surely die,
and when I'm dead and buried,
Susanna, don't you cry.
O, Susanna,
o, don't you cry for me ...

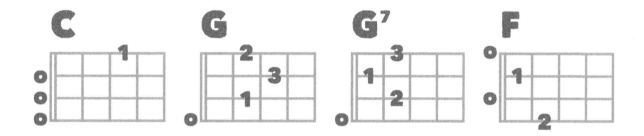

When the saints go marchin' in

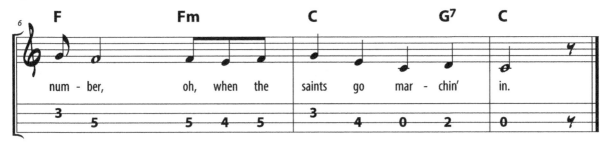

2. And when the stars begin to shine ...

3. And when the band begins to play ...

4. When Gabriel blows in his horn ...

5. And when the sun refuses to shine ...

6. And when they crown Him Lord of Lords ...

7. And on that halleluja-day ...

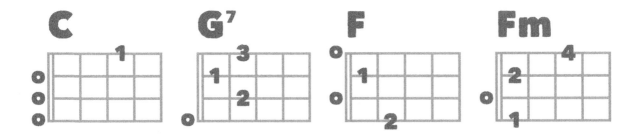

We wish you a merry Christmas

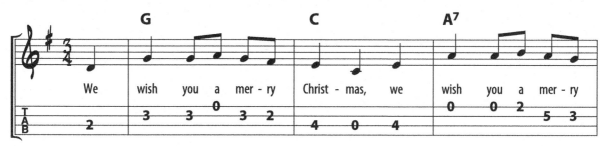

2. Now bring us some figgy pudding (3x)
   And bring some out here!

3. For we all like figgy pudding,
   We all like figgy pudding (2x)
   So bring some out here!

4. And we won't go until we've got some,
   We won't go until we've got some (2x)
   So bring some out here!

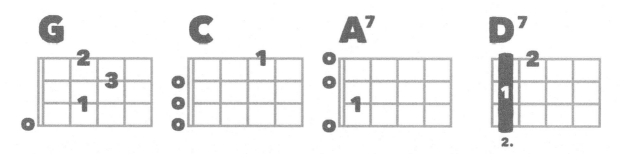

My Bonnie lies over the ocean

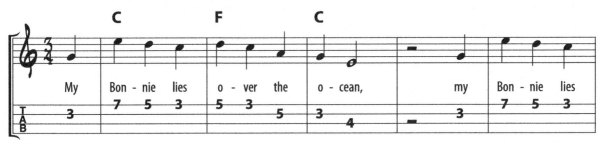

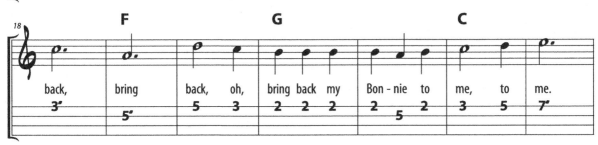

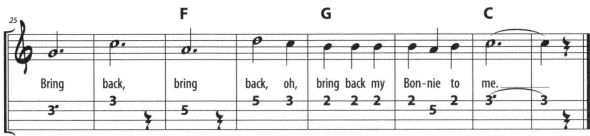

2. *Last night as I lay on my pillow,*
   last night as I lay on my bed.
   Last night as I lay on my pillow,
   I dreamed that my Bonnie was dead,
   Bring back, bring back,
   bring back my Bonnie to me, to me.
   Bring back, bring back,
   bring back my Bonnie to me.

3. *Oh blow ye the winds o'er the ocean,*
   and blow ye the winds o'er the sea.
   Oh blow ye the winds o'er the ocean,
   and bring back my Bonnie to me.
   Bring back, bring back,
   bring back my Bonnie to me, to me.
   Bring back, bring back,
   bring back my Bonnie to me.

4. *The winds have blown over the ocean,*
   the winds have blown over the sea.
   The winds have blown over the ocean,
   and brought back my Bonnie to me.
   Bring back, bring back,
   bring back my Bonnie to me, to me.
   Bring back, bring back,
   bring back my Bonnie to me.

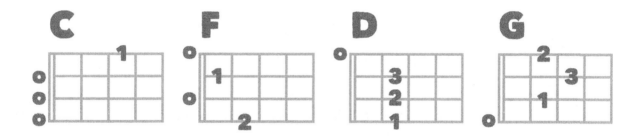

Good night, Ladies

2. Farewell, ladies! (3x)
   We're going to leave you now.
   Merrily we roll along,
   roll along, roll along,
   merrily we roll along,
   o'er the deep blue sea.

3. Sweet dreams, ladies! (3x)
   We're going to leave you now.
   Merrily we roll along,
   roll along, roll along,
   merrily we roll along,
   o'er the deep blue sea.

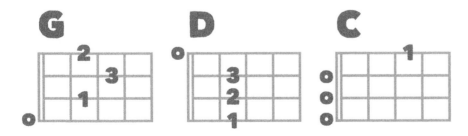

Tom Dooley

2. *This time tomorrow,*
   Reckon where I'll be?
   If it hadn't been for Grayson,
   I'd a-been in Tennesse.

3. *This time tomorrow,*
   Reckon where I'll be?
   Down in some lonesome valley,
   Hangin' from a white oak tree.

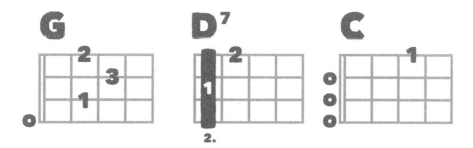

Row, row, row

C

Row, row, row your boat, gent - ly down the stream.

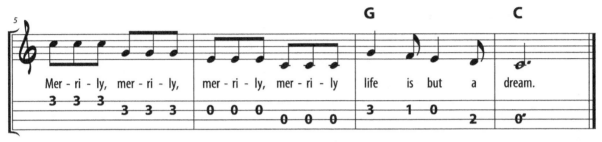

G   C

Mer - ri - ly, mer - ri - ly, mer - ri - ly, mer - ri - ly life is but a dream.

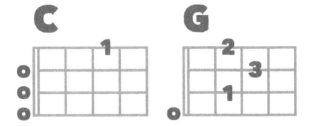

C   G

Kum ba yah

2. Someone's crying, Lord, kum ba yah!

3. Someone's singing, Lord, kum ba yah!

4. Someone's praying, Lord, kum ba yah!

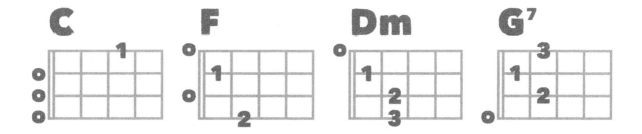

Humpty Dumpty

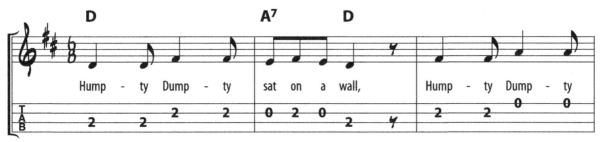

Hump – ty Dump – ty sat on a wall, Hump – ty Dump – ty

had a great fall. All the king's hors – es and all the king's men

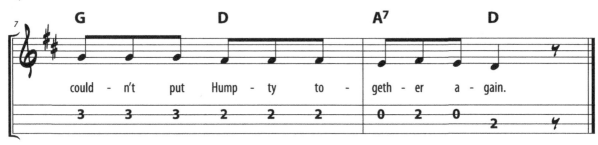

could – n't put Hump – ty to – geth – er a – gain.

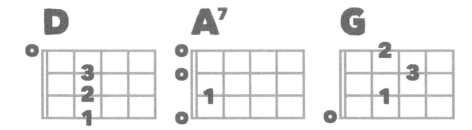

Jack Sprat

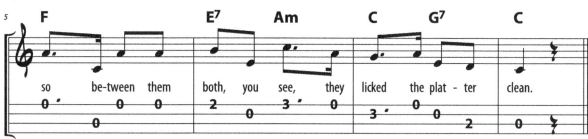

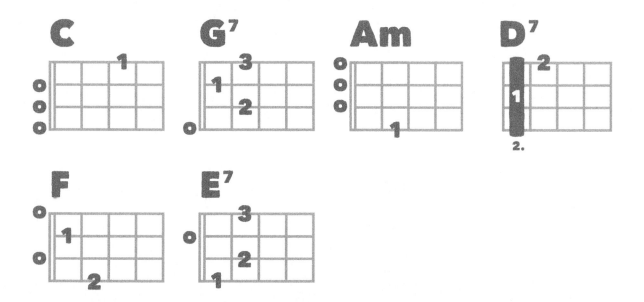

Mary had a little lamb

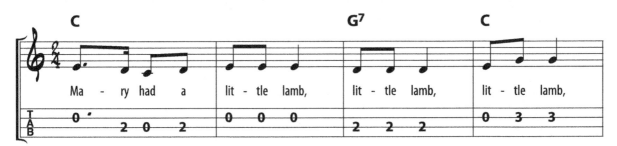

2. And everywhere that Mary went,
   Mary went, Mary went,
   everywhere that Mary went
   the lamb was sure to go.

3. It followed her to school one day,
   school one day, school one day,
   it followed her to school one day
   which was against the rule.

4. It made the children laugh and play,
   laugh and play, laugh and play,
   it made the children laugh and play
   to see a lamb at school.

5. And so the teacher turned it out,
   turned it out, turned it out,
   and so the teacher turned it out
   but still it lingered near.

6. And waited patiently about,
   Patiently, patiently,
   and waited patiently about
   till Mary did appear.

7. "Why does the lamb love Mary so,
   Mary so, Mary so?"
   "Why does the lamb love Mary so?"
   the eager children cry.

8. "Because the lamb loves Mary so,
   Mary so, Mary so",
   "Because the lamb loves Mary so",
   the teacher did reply.

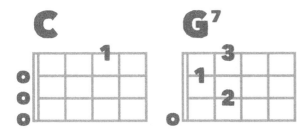

Six little ducks

2. Down to the river they would go,
   Wibble, wobble, wibble, wobble, to and fro.
   But the one little duck with the feather on his back,
   he led the others with a quack, quack, quack
   Quack, quack, quack, quack, quack, quack,
   he led the others with a quack, quack, quack.

3. Back from the river they would come,
   Wibble, wobble, wibble, wobble, ho, hum, hum.
   But the one little duck with the feather on his back,
   he led the others with a quack, quack, quack.
   Quack, quack, quack, quack, quack, quack,
   he led the others with a quack, quack, quack.

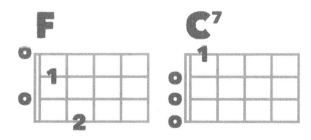

One, two, buckle my shoe

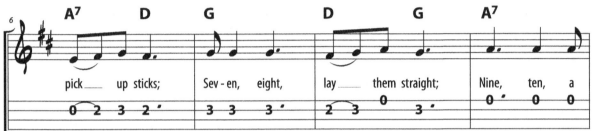

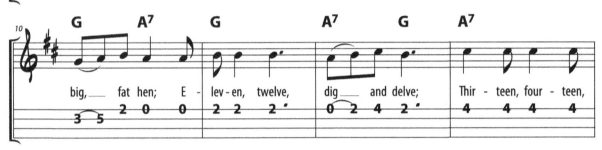

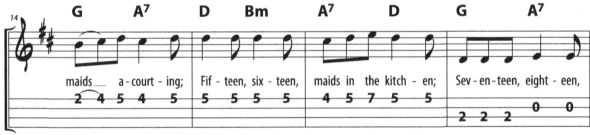

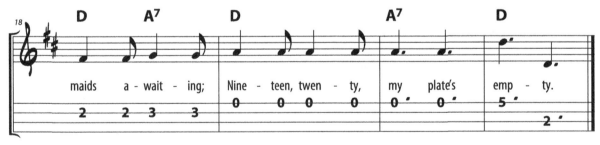

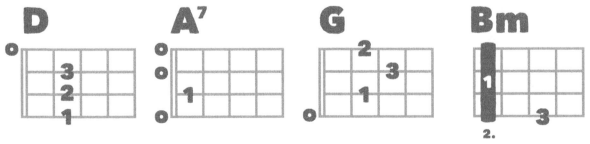

The Hokey Pokey

You put your right hand in, you put your right hand out, you put your

right hand in, and you shake it all a-bout. You

do the ho-key po-key, and you turn your-self a-round,

that what it's all a bout!

You put your left hand in ...
You put your right foot in ...
You put your left foot in ...
You put your right shoulder in ...
You put your left shoulder in ...

You put your right hip in ...
You put your left hip in ...
You put your head in ...
You put your whole self in ...

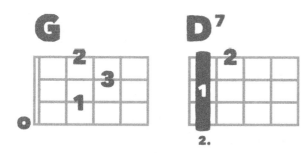

Georgie Porgie

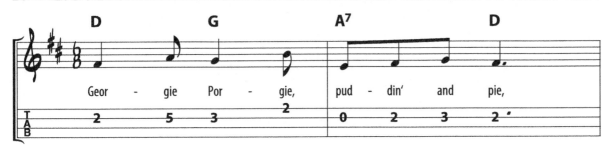

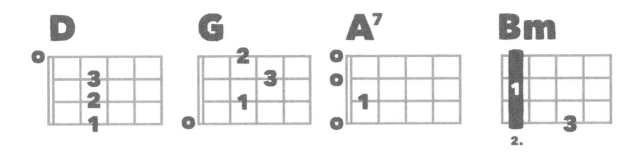

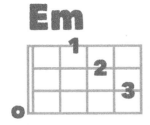

Jack be nimble

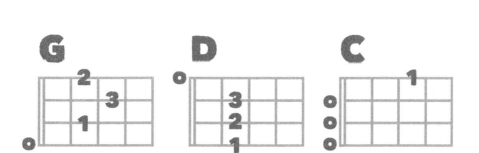

Mulberry bush

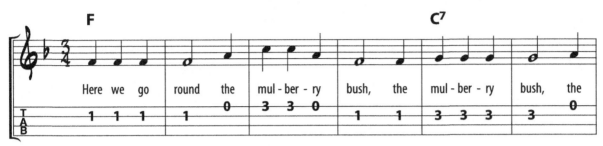

Here we go round the mul-ber-ry bush, the mul-ber-ry bush, the

mul-ber-ry bush. Here we go round the mul-ber-ry bush so ear-ly

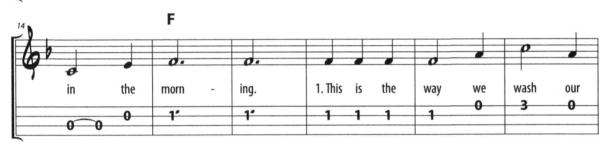

in the morn - ing. 1. This is the way we wash our

face, we wash our face, we wash our face. This is the

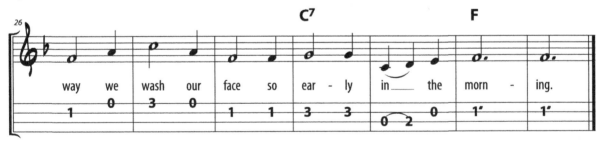

way we wash our face so ear-ly in___ the morn - ing.

2. This is the way we wash our face,
   we wash our face, we wash our face.
   This is the way we wash our face
   so early in the morning.

3. This is the way we comb our hair,
   we comb our hair, we comb our hair.
   This is the way we comb our hair
   so early in the morning.

4. This is the way we brush our teeth,
   we brush our teeth, we brush our teeth.
   This is the way we brush our teeth
   so early in the morning.

5. This is the way we put on our clothes,
   we put on our clothes, we put on our clothes.
   This is the way we put on our clothes
   so early in the morning.

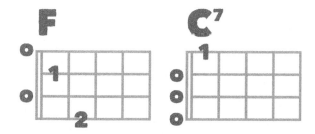

The farmer in the dell

The farm - er in the dell, the far - mer in the dell,

heigh - ho, the der - ry - o, the farm - er in the dell.

2. The farmer takes the wife (2×)
   Heigh-ho, the derry-o …
   The farmer takes the wife

3. The wife takes the child (2×)
   Heigh-ho, the derry-o …
   The wife takes the child

4. The child takes the nurse (2×)
   Heigh-ho, the derry-o …
   The child takes the nurse

5. The nurse takes the cow (2×)
   Heigh-ho, the derry-o …
   The nurse takes the cow

6. The cow takes the dog (2×)
   Heigh-ho, the derry-o …
   The cow takes the dog

7. The dog takes the cat (2×)
   Heigh-ho, the derry-o …
   The dog takes the cat

8. The cat takes the mouse (2×)
   Heigh-ho, the derry-o …
   The cat takes the mouse

9. The mouse takes the cheese (2×)
   Heigh-ho, the derry-o …
   The mouse takes the cheese

10. The cheese stands alone (2×)
    Heigh-ho, the derry-o …
    The cheese stands alone

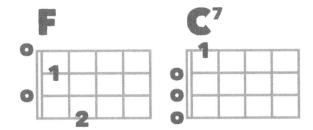

Bye, baby bunting

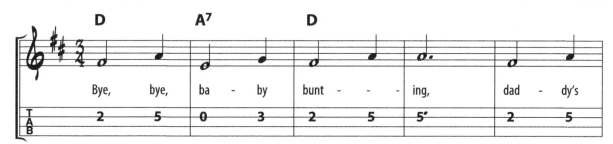

Bye, bye, ba - by bunt - - - ing, dad - dy's

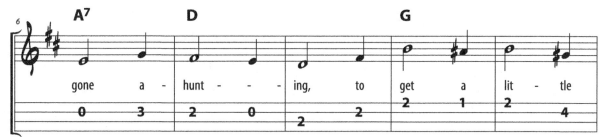

gone a - hunt - - ing, to get a lit - tle

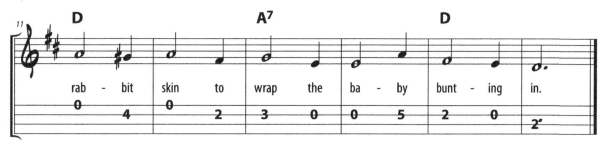

rab - bit skin to wrap the ba - by bunt - ing in.

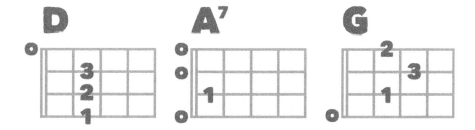

Lucy Locket

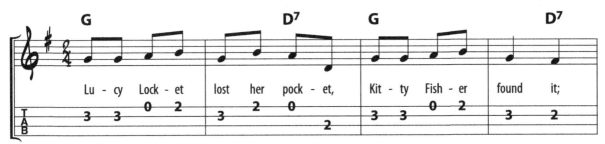

Lu - cy Lock - et | lost her pock - et, | Kit - ty Fish - er | found it;

not a pen - ny | was there in it, | on - ly rib - bon | 'round it.

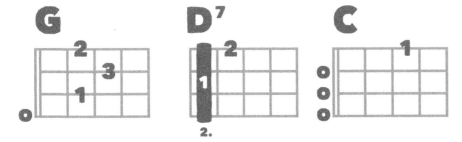

G   D7   C

Pease porridge hot

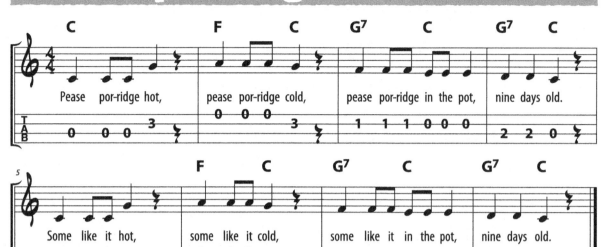

Pease por-ridge hot, pease por-ridge cold, pease por-ridge in the pot, nine days old.

Some like it hot, some like it cold, some like it in the pot, nine days old.

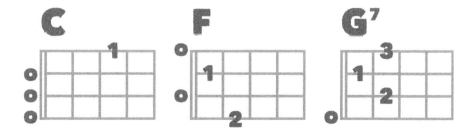

Nobody likes me

No - bod - y likes me, ev - 'ry - bod - y hates me, guess I'll go eat worms.

Long, thin, slim - y ones, short, fat, juic - y ones, it - sy, bit - sy, fuz - zy, wuz - zy worms.

2. *Down goes the first one,*
   down goes the second one,
   oh, how they wiggle and squirm.
   Long, thin, slimy ones,
   short, fat, juicy ones
   itsy, bitsy, fuzzy, wuzzy worms.

3. *Up comes the first one,*
   up come the second one,
   oh, how they wiggle and squirm.
   Long, thin, slimy ones,
   short, fat, juicy ones,
   itsy, bitsy, fuzzy, wuzzy worms.

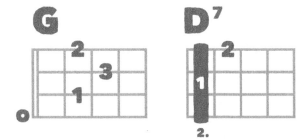

Little Miss Muffet

Lit - tle Miss Muff - et   sat on a tuf - fet,   eat - ing her curds   and

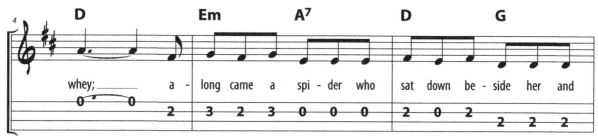

whey;____   a - long came a spi - der who   sat down be - side her and

fright - ened Miss Muff - et a - way.____

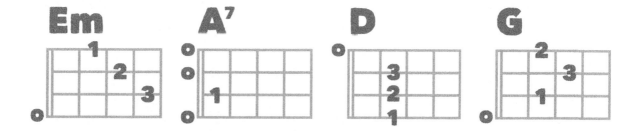

Pat-a-cake

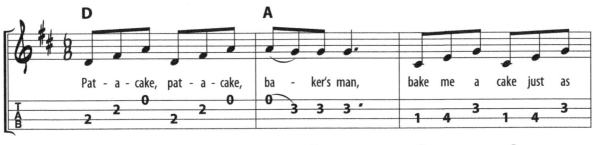

Pat - a - cake, pat - a - cake, ba - ker's man, bake me a cake just as

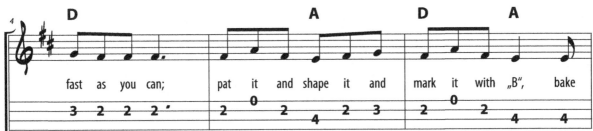

fast as you can; pat it and shape it and mark it with „B", bake

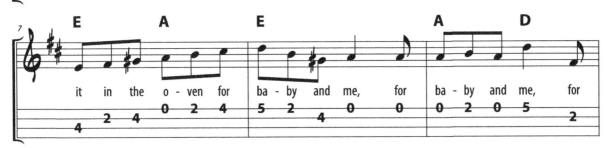

it in the o - ven for ba - by and me, for ba - by and me, for

ba - by and me, bake it in the o - ven for ba - by and me.

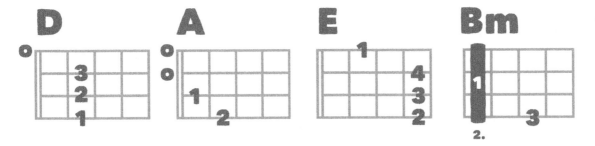

Peter, Peter, pumpkin eater

2. Peter, Peter pumpkin eater,
   had another and didn't love her;
   Peter learned to read and spell,
   and then he loved her very well.

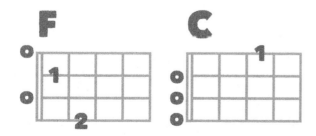

There was a crooked man

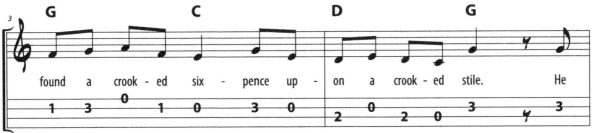

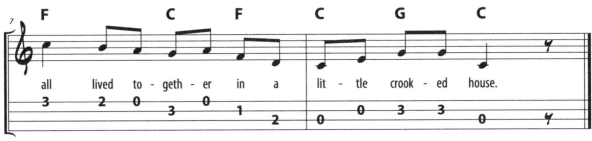

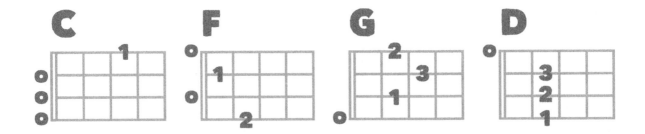

Lazy Mary

2. No, no, mother I won't get up,
   I won't get up, I won't get up,
   No, no, mother I won't get up,
   I won't get up today.

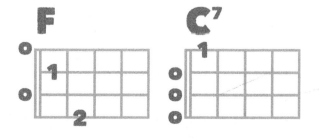

Over in the meadow

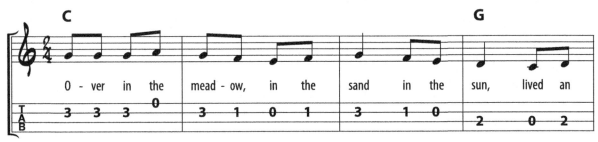

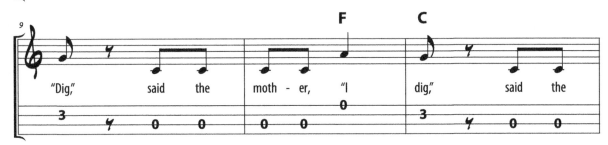

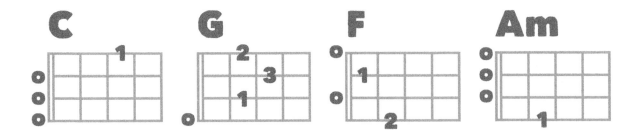

2. Over in the meadow where the stream runs blue,
    lived an old mother fish and her little fishies two.
    "Swim," said the mother, "We swim," said the two,
    so they swam and they swam where the stream runs blue.

3. Over in the meadow in a hole in the tree,
    Lived an old mother owl and her little owls three.
    "Whoo," said the mother, "We whoo," said the three,
    so they whooed and they whoeed in the hole in the tree.

4. Over in the meadow by the old barn door,
    Lived an old mother rat and her little ratties four.
    "Gnaw," said the mother, "We gnaw," said the four,
    so they gnawed and the gnawed by the old barn door.

5. Over in the meadow in a snug beehive,
    Lived an old mother bee and her little bees five.
    "Buzz," said the mother, "We buzz," said the five,
    so they buzzed and they buzzed in the snug beehive.

6. Over in the meadow in a nest built of sticks,
    Lived an old mother crow and her little crows six.
    "Caw," said the mother, "We caw," said the six,
    so they cawed and the cawed in the nest built of sticks.

7. Over in the meadow where the grass grows so even,
    Lived an old mother frog and her little froggies seven.
    "Jump," said the mother, "We jump," said the seven,
    so they jumped and they jumped where the grass grows so even.

8. Over in the meadow by the old mossy gate,
    Lived an old mother lizard and her little lizards eight.
    "Bask," said the mother, "We bask," said the eight,
    so they basked and they basked by the old mossy gate.

9. Over in the meadow by the old scotch pine,
    Lived an old mother duck and her little duckies nine.
    "Quack," said the mother, "We quack," said the nine,
    so they quacked and they quacked by the old scotch pine.

10. Over in the meadow in a cozy, wee den,
    Lived an old mother beaver and her little beavers ten.
    "Beave," said the mother, "We beave," said the ten,
    so they beaved and they beaved in their cozy, wee den.

Three little kittens

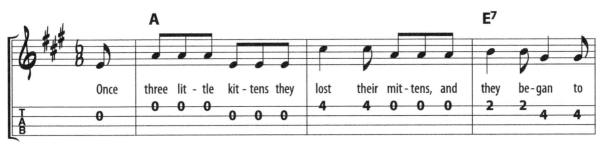

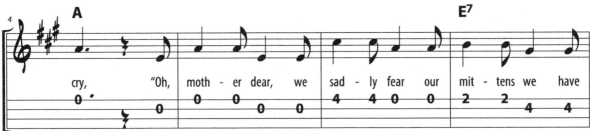

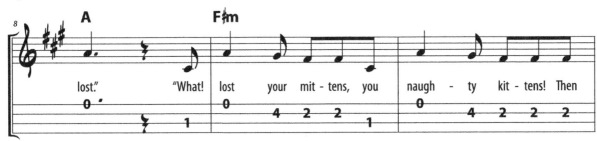

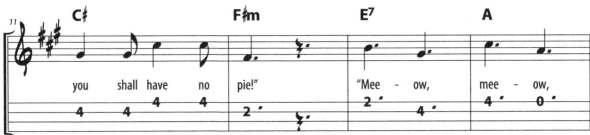

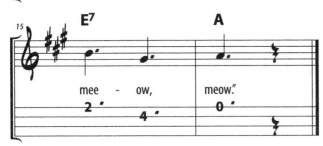

2. The three little kittens they found their mittens,
   and they began to cry,
   "Oh, mother dear, see here, see here,
   we have found our mittens."
   "Put on your mittens, you silly kittens,
   and you shall have some pie."
   "Mee-ow, mee-ow, mee-ow."

3. The three little kittens put on their mittens,
   and soon ate up the pie;
   "Oh, mother dear, we greatly fear
   we have soiled our mittens."
   "What! soiled your mittens, you naughty kittens!"
   Then they began to sigh,
   "Mee-ow, mee-ow, mee-ow."

4. The three little kittens they washed their mittens,
   and hung them out to dry;
   "Oh! mother dear, do you not hear,
   we have washed our mittens."
   "What! washed your mittens, then you're good kittens,
   But I smell a rat close by."
   "Mee-ow, mee-ow, mee-ow."

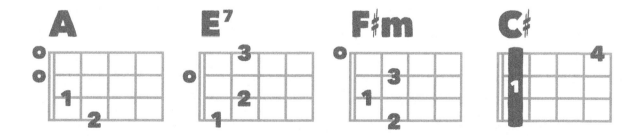

Animal fair

I went to the an - i - mal fair, the birds and beasts were there,

the big ba - boon, by the light of the moon was comb-ing his au - burn hair.

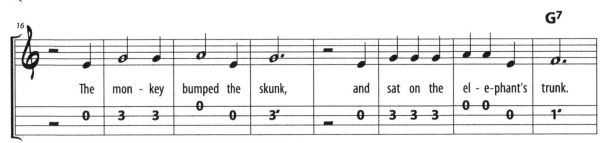

The mon - key bumped the skunk, and sat on the el - e-phant's trunk.

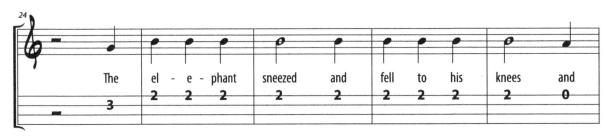

The el - e - phant sneezed and fell to his knees and

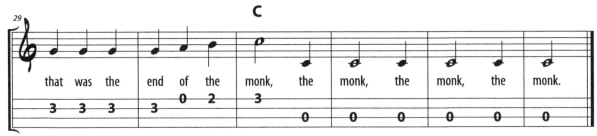

that was the end of the monk, the monk, the monk, the monk.

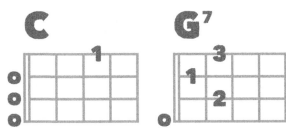

See-saw, Margery Daw

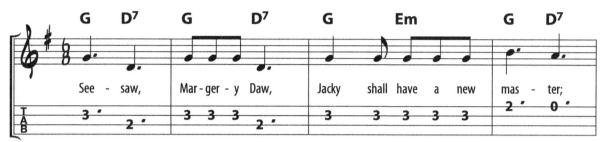

See - saw, Mar-ger-y Daw, Jacky shall have a new mas - ter;

Jacky shall earn but a pen-ny a day, be-cause he can't work an-y fas - ter.

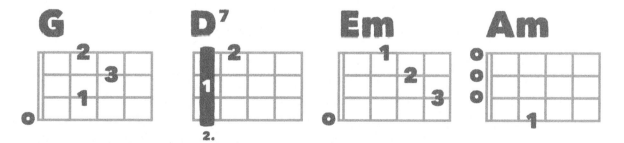

Hot cross buns

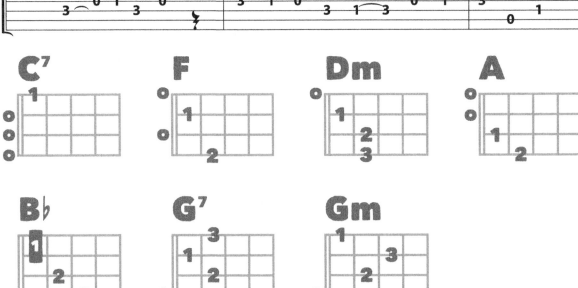

Five little ducks

2. Four little ducks went swimming one day,
   over the hill and far away.
   The mother duck said "Quack, quack, quack, quack",
   and only three little ducks came back.

3. Three little ducks went swimming one day,
   over the hill and far away.
   The mother duck said "Quack, quack, quack, quack",
   and only two little ducks came back.

4. Two little ducks went swimming one day,
   over the hill and far away.
   The mother duck said "Quack, quack, quack, quack",
   and only one little duck came back.

5. One little ducks went swimming one day,
   over the hill and far away.
   The mother duck said "Quack, quack, quack, quack",
   and all the five little ducks came back.

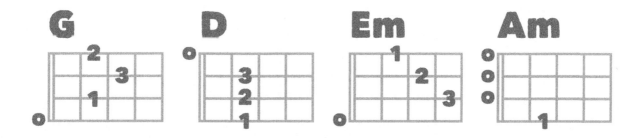

All the pretty little horses

Hush - a - bye, don't you cry; go to sleep-y, lit - tle ba - by.

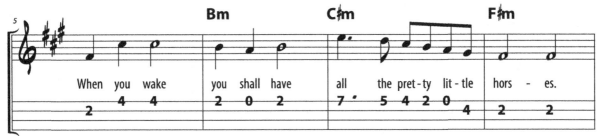

When you wake you shall have all the pret-ty lit-tle hors - es.

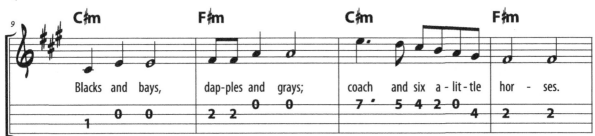

Blacks and bays, dap-ples and grays; coach and six a-lit-tle hor - ses.

Hush - a - bye, don't you cry; go to sleep-y, lit - tle ba - by.

2. *Hush-a-bye, don't you cry; go to sleepy, little baby.*
When you wake you shall have all the pretty little horses.
Paint and Bay, sorrel and gray, all the pretty little ponies.
Hush-a-bye, don't you cry; go to sleepy, little baby.

3. *Hush-a-bye, don't you cry; go to sleepy, little baby.*
When you wake you shall have all the pretty little horses.
Way down under the meadow lies a poor little lambie.
Hush-a-bye, don't you cry; go to sleepy, little baby.

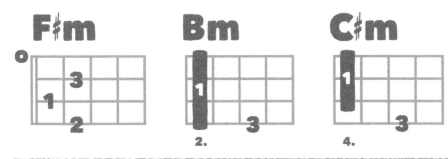

(How to read) Chord diagrams

Horizontal lines represent the strings of the Ukulele, vertical lines the frets.

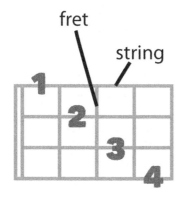

The fingers of the fretting hand are numbered 1-4:
1 = Index finger
2 = Middle finger
3 = Ringfinger
4 = Little finger (pinky)

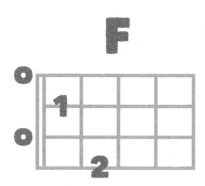

The chord symbol is given above the chord.

Open strings are indicated by an "0" to the left of the diagram, muted strings (strings that are not played or damped) by an "x".

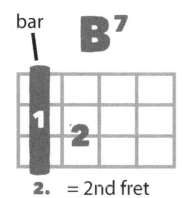

Fretboard positions are indicated below the chord. If a chord is to be played as a so-called bar chord (i.e. fretting more than one string with the same finger) this is indicated by a black bar. The number inside the bar indicates the recommended fretting finger.

Tuning the Ukulele

The strings of the Ukulele are numbered 1-4 (starting with the one next to the floor).

1st string	=	A
2nd string	=	E
3rd string	=	C
4th string	=	G

In contrast to most other string instruments, the strings of the Ukulele are tuned in what is called a reentrant tuning (meaning the lowest tuned string of the instrument is not the bottom string). This can make tuning the instrument slightly confusing, especially for beginners.
There are lots of ways to tune your Ukulele, one of which is shown below in graphical form.

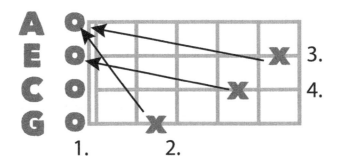

This reads as follows:

1. First tune the G string using a reference tone from another instrument (like a piano) or a tuner.
2. Fret the G string at the 2. fret. Play and compare to the open (not fretted) A string. Tune the A string until both pitches match exactly.
3. Fret the E string at the 5. Fret. Play and compare to the open A string. Tune the E string until both pitches match.
4. Finally, fret the C string at the 4. Fret. Play and compare to the open E string.

Tune the E string until both pitches match.

PS. Of course, using an (electronic) tuner is a great way to tune tour Ukulele, too.

Basic chords

On the following pages I've compiled the chords used in this book. I've also included some chords you'll probably encounter in other books. Naturally, this chord collection is far from complete – there are literally thousands of Ukulele chords (some common, some pretty obscure). If you want to expand your chord repertoire (or simply look up a chord you don't know), a chord chart is always a wise investment, and of course you can find almost any Ukulele chord on the internet.

Depending on the musical context, some chords may have more than one name:

$$C\sharp = D\flat, \quad D\sharp = E\flat, \quad F\sharp = G\flat, \quad G\sharp = A\flat \quad und \quad A\sharp = B\flat$$

For Ukulele players this simply means: C♯ and D♭ are played the same and they sound the same. If, for example, you happen to stumble upon a G♯m (G sharp minor) chord, don't worry: just play A♭m.

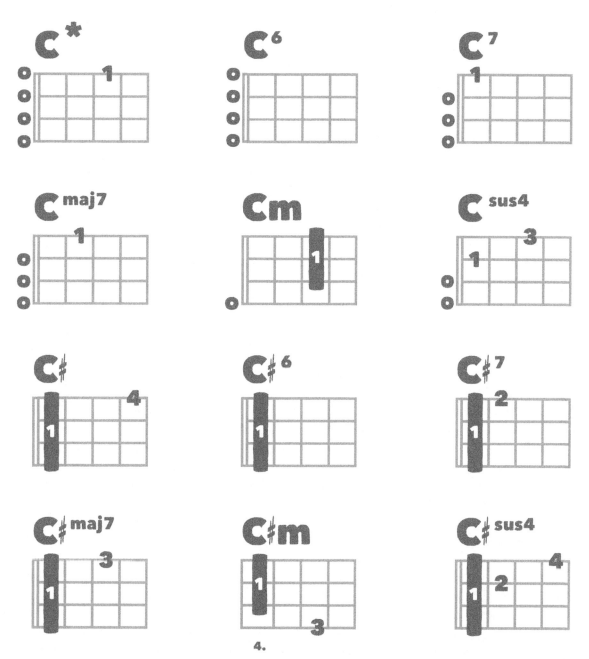

* = Alternate fingering for this chord: ring finger (3)

Basic chords

D
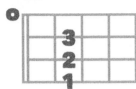

D⁶
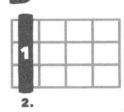
2.

D⁷

2.

Dmaj7
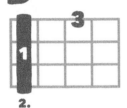
2.

Dm
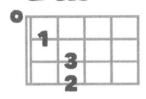

Dsus4
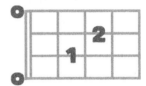

E♭

E♭⁶
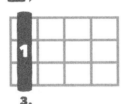
3.

E♭⁷
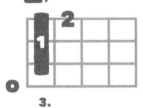
3.

E♭maj7
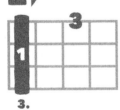
3.

E♭m

E♭7/sus4
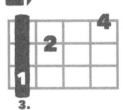
3.

E
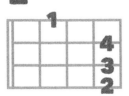

E⁶
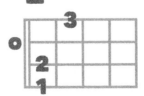

E⁷

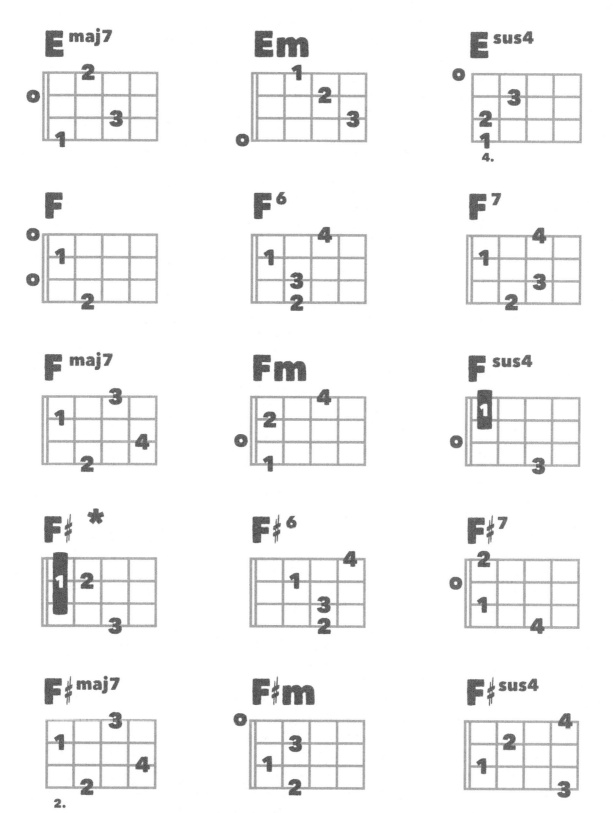

* = This chord can also be played as a full bar chord.

Basic chords

G

G 6
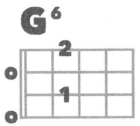

G 7
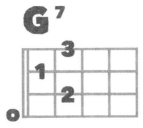

G maj7
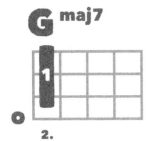
2.

Gm
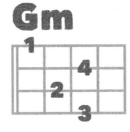

G sus4
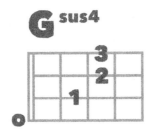

A♭
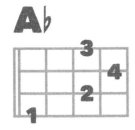

A♭ 6
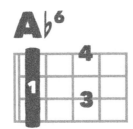

A♭ 7
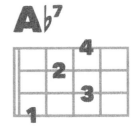

A♭ maj7
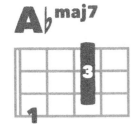

A♭m
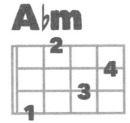

A♭ sus4
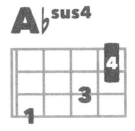

A
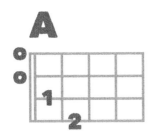

A 6
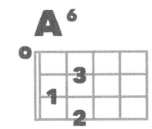

A 7
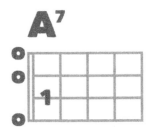

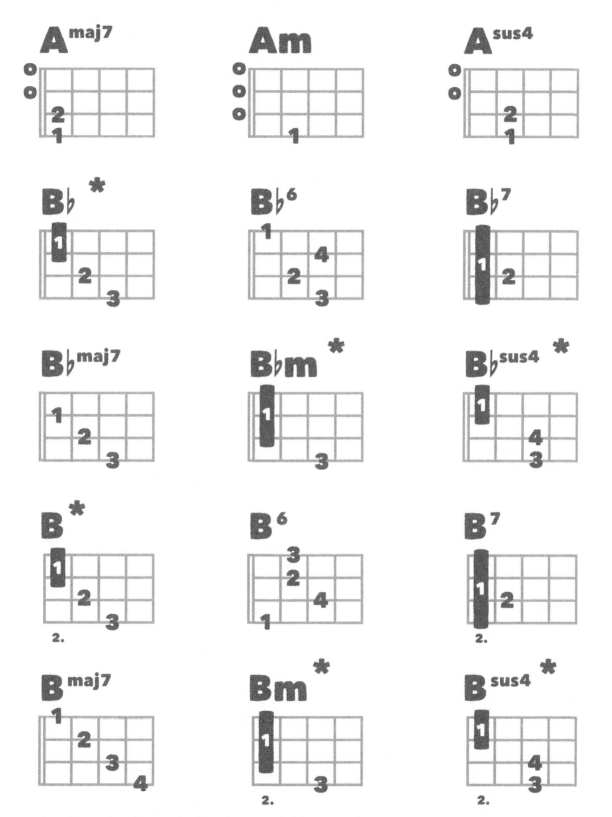

* = These chords can also be played as full bar chords.

Strumming patterns

The following is a selection of basic strumming pattern which you can use for song accompaniment. These are just for starters - you'll soon use other, more elaborate pattern or invent your own. Feel free to use a pick or your finger(s) for strumming – basically whatever feels best.

Here's how they're read:

- The horizontal lines represent the strings of your Ukulele.
  Downstroke (strumming in the direction of the floor): arrow upward
  Upstroke: arrow downward.
- The length of the arrows indicates which strings to strum.
- Each of these pattern shows a whole measure.

For song accompaniment you can choose (and also combine) whatever pattern feels best to you, but keep in mind to match the pattern's time to the time of the song, e.g. for a song in 4/4 time only use strumming patterns in 4/4 time.
Songs in 2/2 time can be played using strumming patterns in 4/4 time.

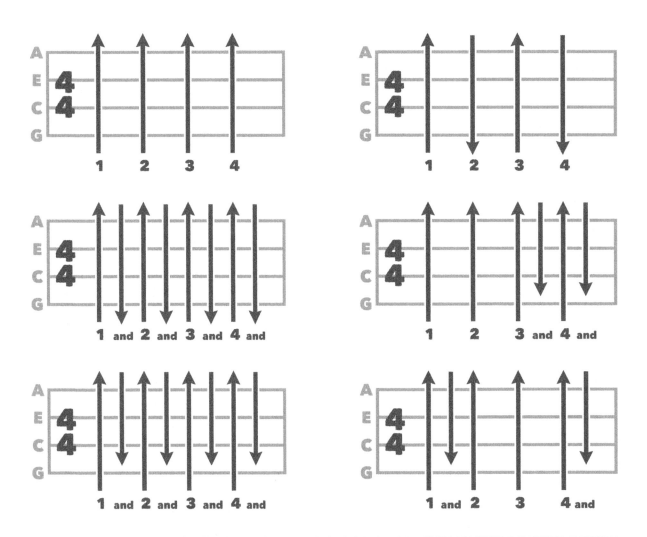

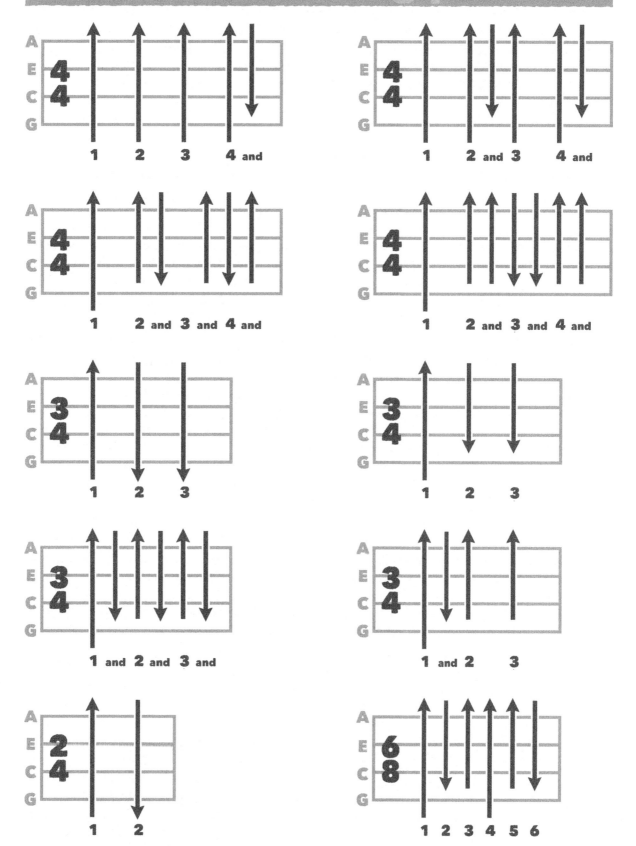

Picking patterns

A lot of songs sound particularly good when played using a picking pattern. Here's the basic idea: instead of picking all the notes of a chord simultaneously with you finger(s) or a pick, you play them successively, one after the other. Picking patterns are commonly used for longer musical sections (or even whole songs) and adapted to the chord changes if necessary. Here's an example, using the G major chord:

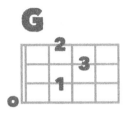

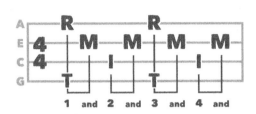

T = thumb
I = index finger
M = middle finger
R = ring finger

As in tablature, horizontal lines represent the strings of your Ukulele. The time signature is notated at the beginning of the pattern as a fraction (here: 4/4; this is a pattern for songs in 4/4 time). The letters T, I, M and R indicate the fingers of the picking hand. Below the pattern I've notated how to count it. Here's a step-by-step explanation of the above example:
- on the first beat ("1") thumb and ring finger simultaneously pick the G string and the A string.
- on the second half of the first beat ("1and") the middle finger picks the E string.
- on the second beat ("2") the index finger picks the C string.
- on the second half of the second beat ("2and") the middle finger picks the E string once again.
This pattern is repeated for the second half of the bar (this isn't always the case).

There are a few basic things to keep in mind when using picking patterns:
Obviously, the pattern's time signature has to match that of the song. In some cases, the pattern has to be adapted to a certain chord or a chord change, but most of the time you can use the following simple rule:
• pick the G string with your thumb,
• the C string with your index finger,
• the E string with your middle finger and
• the A string with your ring finger.

One of the best ways to practise picking patterns is to play them on open strings until the movement of your fingers becomes second nature – practicing this way ensures you'll be able to concentrate on more important things when it's time to play the song.
When the picking pattern has been "automized" to a certain degree it's time to add chords and chord changes. Take your time because nothing sounds worse than a "stuttering" picking pattern interfering with a smooth chord change.
On the following pages you'll find some basic picking patterns to choose from. Of course, this is just a small selection from the multitude of possible patterns, meant to whet your appetite – you'll soon find varying patterns and inventing new ones of your own can be lots of fun!

For a start, you may want to try:
• Combining different picking patterns
  (e. g. one for the verse and one for the chorus).
• Combining picking patterns with strumming patterns.
• Mixing picking patterns with melody lines and damping techniques.
• Playing some of your favorites "backwards".

Sometimes you'll encounter indications in Spanish:
P (pulgar) = thumb
I (indice) = index finger
M (medio) = middle finger
A (anular) = ring finger

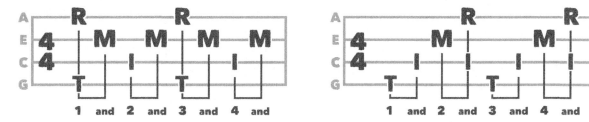
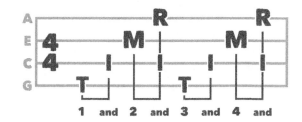

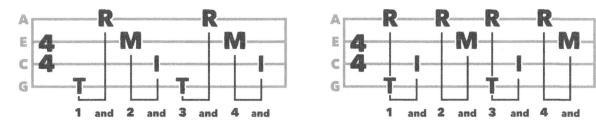
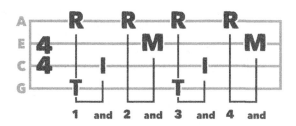

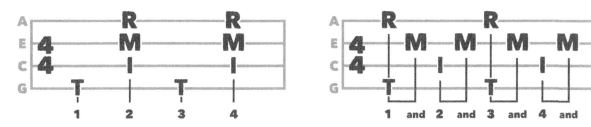
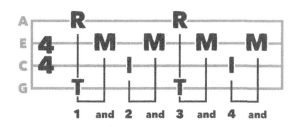

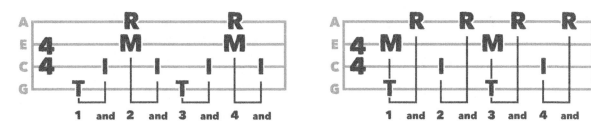
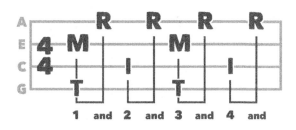

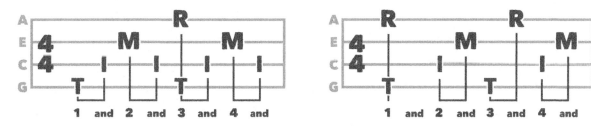
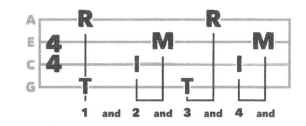

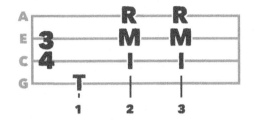

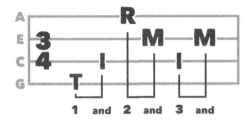

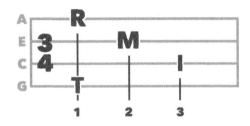

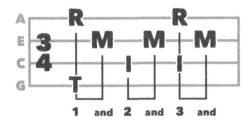

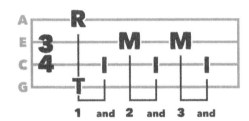

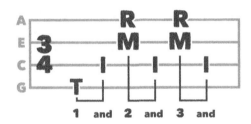

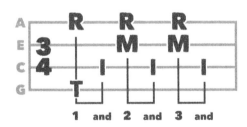

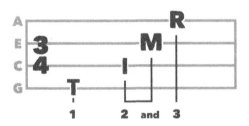

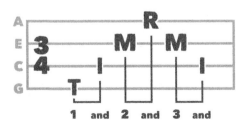

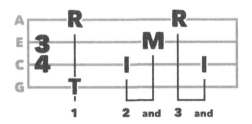

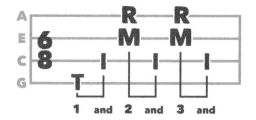

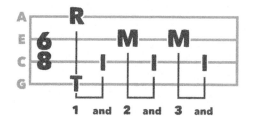

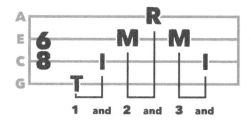

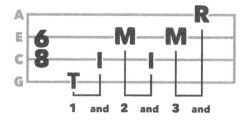

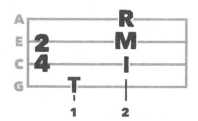

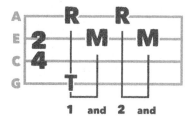

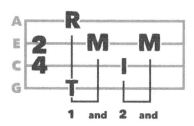

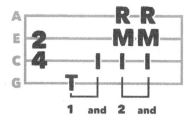

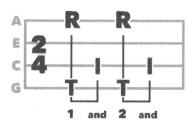

Ukulele Songbooks
by Thomas Balinger

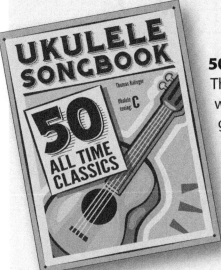

50 All time classics
This book features 50 songs known and loved the world over, arranged for Ukulele. From „Amazing grace" and „Camptown races" to Banks of the Ohio" or Scarborough fair": songs every Ukulele player simply has to know!

50 All time classics, Vol. II
The follow-up to the successful "Ukulele Classics" songbook, this handy collection contains another 50 great songs, arranged for easy Ukulele in C (G-C-E-A).

Best of Gospel
Who doesn't know famous Gospel songs like "When the saints go marchin' in" or "Down by the riverside"? But hold on – there's more to Gospel than just the "hits"!

Made in the USA
Monee, IL
10 January 2021